Back Roads of Washington

Rt. 1 Box 444
GEO. L. YARNELL

Seen near
BZ Corners,
Klickitat County

Books by Earl Thollander

BACK ROADS OF NEW ENGLAND
BACK ROADS OF OREGON
BACK ROADS OF WASHINGTON
BACK ROADS OF CALIFORNIA
EARL THOLLANDER'S BACK ROADS
   OF CALIFORNIA
BACK ROADS OF THE CAROLINAS
SCENIC BYWAYS OF ARIZONA
EARL THOLLANDER'S
   SAN FRANCISCO

Farm on Lopez Island,
San Juan County

Back Roads of Washington

by Earl Thollander

74 Trips on
Washington's
Scenic Byways

Updated Edition

SASQUATCH BOOKS
SEATTLE

I dedicate this book to Diana Klemin

Front cover: The old lighthouse at Marrowstone Point, Jefferson County

Copyright ©1992 by Earl Thollander.
Updated Edition.
Second printing, 1994.

Originally published in 1981 by Clarkson N. Potter, Inc.

Cover illustration by Earl Thollander

Library of Congress Cataloging in Publication Data

Thollander, Earl.
      Back roads of Washington : 74 trips on Washington's scenic byways / by Earl Thollander. — Updated ed.
        p.   cm.
      ISBN: 0-912365-56-0 : $12.95
        1. Washington (State) — Guidebooks. 2. Automobile travel — Washington (State)—Guidebooks. 3. Washington (State)—History, Local.   I. Title.
F889.3. T48 1992
917.9704'43—dc20
                               91-45768
                               CIP

ISBN: 0-912365-56-0

Note: Anyone noticing discrepancies in the maps or changes in roads is invited to write the author at 19210 Highway 128, Calistoga, California 94515.

Published by Sasquatch Books
1008 Western Avenue
Seattle, Washington 98104
(206) 467-4300

4

Grain elevator at Marlin, Grant County

Contents

9   Foreword by Willard R. Espy

10 Preface

11 Author's Note

Back Roads of Southwestern Washington

12 Map of Southwestern Washington

13 Introduction to Southwestern Washington

14 Clark County back roads

16 The road to Hulda Klager's house

18 Willow Grove loop trip along the Columbia River

21 The road along Steamboat Slough

22 Grays River Covered Bridge road

25 Back road to Tsako-te-hahsh-eetl

29 The road to Bay Center

31 A road through Willapa country

32 Rainbow Falls and Boistfort roads

37 The back road to see Puyallup and Tahoma glaciers

40 Back road from Eatonville

44 The road to Wilkeson and Mowich Lake

Back Roads of Northwestern Washington

46 Map of Northwestern Washington

47 Introduction to Northwestern Washington

48 Lake Quinault rain forest road

51 The Queets Corridor Road

55 The road to the mouth of the Quillayute

57 Lake Ozette back road

59 The road to Cape Flattery

60 The road to Obstruction Point

65 Deer Park Road to Blue Mountain

67   The road from Port Gamble

69   A trip to Marrowstone Island

70   Road to Port Townsend

71   Fort Casey to Coupeville and Oak Harbor

73   Back road on Lopez Island

76   Orcas Island Road

79   Roads of San Juan

80   Road to La Conner and Mount Vernon

83   Samish Bay road

85   The road to Lynden

89   Roads around Lynden

90   The road to Border House

93   The road to Mount Baker

94   Back road from Sultan to Snohomish

99   Road to Granite Falls

Back Roads of Northeastern Washington

100 Map of Northeastern Washington

101 Introduction to Northeastern Washington

103 Wenatchee Alpine back road

105 East Wenatchee to Chelan

107 Chelan Butte Road

108 Entiat River Road to Chelan

111 The road to Twisp and Winthrop

117 Back road from Winthrop

118 Methow Valley road

120 The road to Sinlahekin Valley

123 Loomis to Nighthawk and Oroville

124 Road to Old Molson and Chesaw

126 Okanogan River road

129 The road through Chewilikan Valley

133 Omak Lake Road

Map legend

. 5.6 . distance in miles between dots

→ → → my route (which may be reversed should you desire)

▲ campgrounds
■ towns and cities
▭ dams
.... rivers, lakes, ferry routes
□ special place
✕ my sketching place
⌂ church
ᴨ picnic grounds
⊞ cemetery
△ mountains
⌂ buildings

NORTH is always toward the top of the page

134 The road to Nespelem and Republic

137 The road past Old Toroda

140 Back roads to and from Northport

143 Road to Orient

145 The road past Deep Lake

146 The back door road to Gardner Cave

148 Road to Manresa Grotto

152 Usk to Chewelah

155 Back road through Colville Valley

156 Back road with two ferry rides across the Columbia River

160 The road to Hartline

162 Back road loop from Coulee City

165 Road along the Spokane River

167 The road through Riverside State Park

Back Roads of Southeastern Washington

168 Map of Southeastern Washington

169 Introduction to Southeastern Washington

171 The road along Hangman Creek

174 Road along Ping Gulch

176 Colfax to Steptoe Butte

178 Country road from Colfax to Pullman

181 The road along Union Flat Creek

182 Four Hollows to Waitsburg

184 Waitsburg to Walla Walla

187 The road to Badger Pocket

190 Farm roads to Fort Simcoe

193 Farm roads along the banks of the Yakima

194 The road to Bickleton and Rock Creek Canyon

196 The road through Goodnoe Hills and Klickitat Valley

199 Back road from White Salmon

200 Epilogue

Yellow
Dandelion

Sketching in Oysterville,
Pacific County

Foreword

Bob Meadows knocked on the door of our cottage and came in before we could answer. "Hey," he said, "there's an artist fellow sittin' out there in the field, just a-drawin' away. I'd sure like to see what he'd do if one of them great big b'ars come up and looked over his shoulder."

As it happens, there are no great big b'ars around Oysterville; ours are middle-sized fellows, though fearsome enough at that. But even if a Kodiak brown bear in all its terrible majesty came visiting, I know what Earl Thollander would do: He would make a place for it in his drawing.

He was sitting out there that rainy day because of me. I had written a book, *Oysterville: Roads to Grandpa's Village,* and Earl had agreed to pretty up the pages with sketches of local sights, animate and inanimate—snipe, oyster shells, falling-down fences, and so on. The way he does.

The way he does is a thing to marvel at. For years, Earl Thollander has been exploring the back roads of this nation, sketching as he goes. His means of transportation is a 1972 Chevrolet pickup truck that serves as both studio and bedroom. At intervals he parks off the road, gets out, and begins to draw. You may have seen him sitting on a rail fence, with his pad in his lap, or leaning forward in a canvas folding chair in a field, as on that day in Oysterville. To find the best vantage point, he sometimes climbs into the branches of a tree or onto the roof of a farmhouse.

Each expedition adds a new installment to a unique pictorial chronicle of America. It is an America invisible from superhighways and absent from headlines. In the America recorded by Earl Thollander you will still find covered bridges, steepled country churches, and barns bursting with hay. You can still pause to marvel over a half-opened jonquil or the cemented nest of a mud swallow. It is an America that has never gone away, but that was forgotten for a while. Now that we are seeking it again, Earl Thollander is pointing out the way.

Should the day come, God forbid, when the last covered bridge and steepled church have vanished, Thollander's elegant drawings will remain as testimony—part of the heritage that they record.

You may fairly accuse me of chauvinism when I say that I admire *Back Roads of Washington* even more than its predecessors. I am, after all, Washingtonian by birth and rearing. But I am right. The two-page drawing of Oysterville is sufficient by itself to make this book immortal.

Willard R. Espy

Oysterville, Washington
January 1981

9

Preface

It has been eleven years since I first explored the back roads of Washington. Fortunately, these scenic byways through the most picturesque places of the state have changed little. In taking these journeys, both you and I can again feel close to the earth — its forests, farms, meadows, wild animals and birds — joyful and at peace with mankind.

Snowbush,
Spokane County

Author's Note

Back Roads of Washington is a nonhighway travel guide through areas of interest and beauty. Each of the book's four parts begins with a sectional map. These will help you locate the back roads on larger maps of Washington State that are available at no charge from many sources, including travel services, chambers of commerce, tourist bureaus, and automobile clubs. Localized maps for all the roads throughout will guide you on specific trips. Unless otherwise indicated, the North Pole is toward the top of the page. Arrows trace my direction of travel, although the routes can easily be reversed. Maps are not to scale because the roads are of varying lengths; however, the mileage notations will provide a sense of their distance. Your odometer will not measure distance exactly the same as mine, but the differences should not be too great. County maps purchased from the Washington State Highway Commission, Department of Transportation, 310 Maple Park Avenue, Olympia, Washington 98504-7300, were essential to me in following the back roads. I also purchased maps at ranger stations when entering forest preserves.

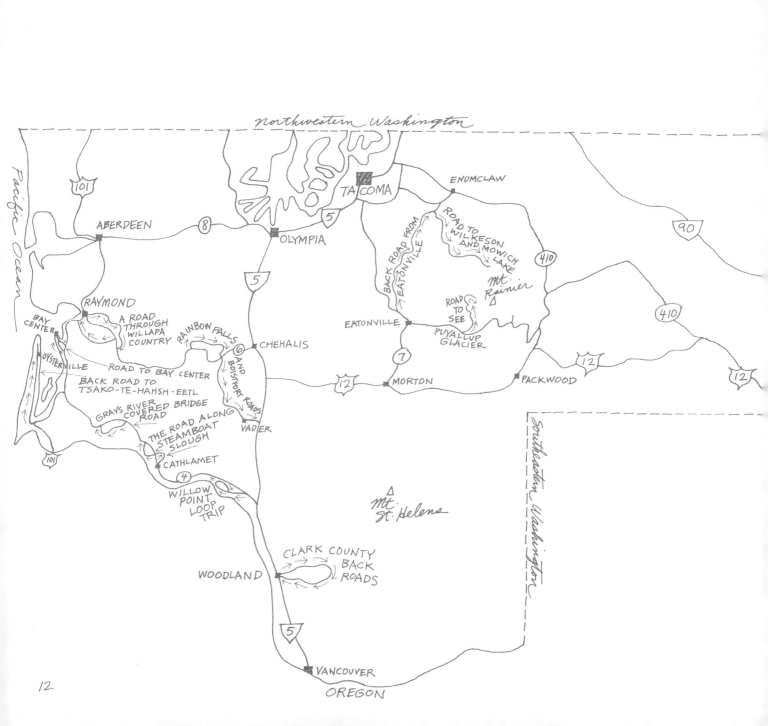

Northwestern Washington

Pacific Ocean

101

ABERDEEN

8

TACOMA

ENUMCLAW

5

OLYMPIA

90

5

RAYMOND

A ROAD THROUGH WILLAPA COUNTRY

RAINBOW FALLS

CHEHALIS

BACK ROAD FROM EATONVILLE

ROAD TO WILKESON AND MOWICH LAKE

410

BAY CENTER

EATONVILLE

ROAD TO SEE

Mt. Rainier

410

OYSTERVILLE

ROAD TO BAY CENTER

AND BOISTFORT ROADS

7

PUYALLUP GLACIER

BACK ROAD TO TSAKO-TE-HAHSH-EETL

12

MORTON

PACKWOOD

12

GRAYS RIVER COVERED BRIDGE ROAD

THE ROAD ALONG STEAMBOAT SLOUGH

VADER

12

101

CATHLAMET

Southeastern Washington

4

WILLOW POINT LOOP TRIP

Mt. St. Helens

CLARK COUNTY BACK ROADS

WOODLAND

5

Vancouver

OREGON

Foxglove, Pierce County

Southwestern Washington

I recall the big foreign-bound cargo ships navigating the bends of the Columbia River; a cool, misty evening while camping at Fort Canby State Park; a fresh fish dinner (perhaps the best I've ever had) at South Bend; snow-topped Mount Rainier glistening in the sunshine, and foxglove blossoming six feet tall.

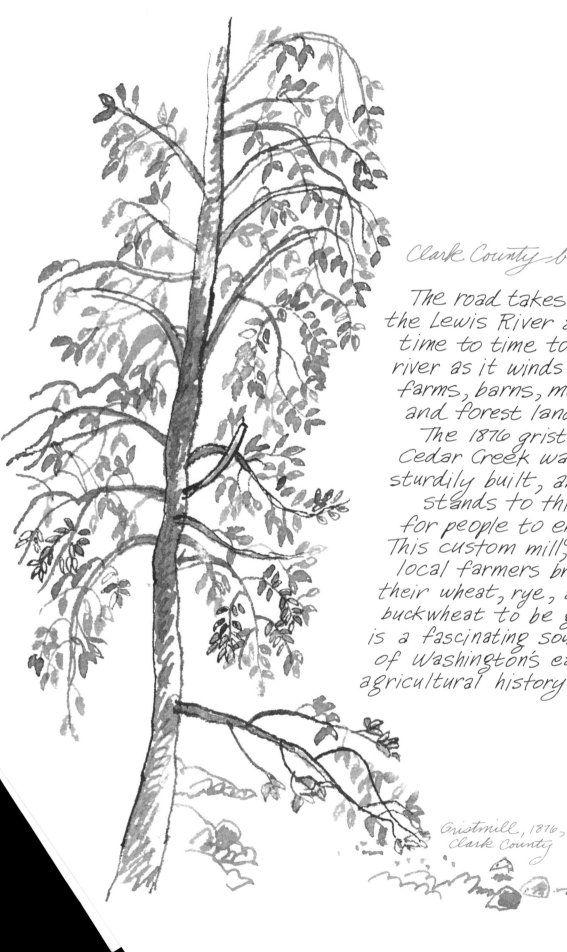

Clark County—back roads

The road takes me across
the Lewis River and from
time to time touches the
river as it winds past
farms, barns, meadows,
and forest land.
  The 1876 gristmill at
Cedar Creek was
sturdily built, and
    stands to this day
  for people to enjoy.
This custom mill, where
local farmers brought
their wheat, rye, and
buckwheat to be ground,
is a fascinating souvenir
of Washington's early
agricultural history.

Gristmill, 1876,
Clark County

15

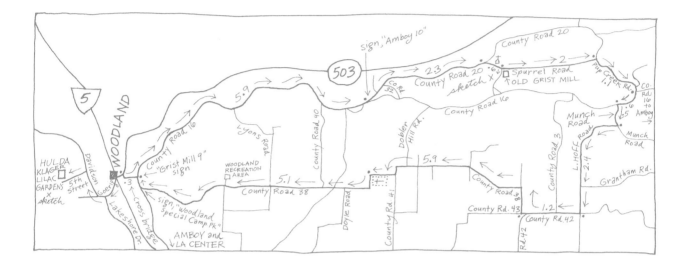

The road to Hulda Klager's house

There are exotic trees and flowers in abundance all around the house of the "Lilac Lady," hybridizer Hulda Klager, in Woodland. The Woodland Federated Garden Club saved the old house and gardens from the bulldozers when she died in 1960 at the age of ninety-six, and the garden club continues to maintain them. Go anytime, but the best season is spring, when you will see the many Klager varieties of lilacs and experience the charm of Hulda's house and garden at its peak. The doll, in my picture from the Klager home, is nicely handmade of lisle cotton stocking material. Grace Davis's rocker dates from about 1880.

Grace Davis's rocker
circa 1880, Hulda Klager
House, Woodland,
Cowlitz county

17

Willow Grove loop trip along the Columbia River

While riding atop dikes one gets views of
pastureland, grazing cows, barns, fishing boats,
log floats, and, of course, the Columbia River
with its big cargo ship traffic on the opposite
shore. The wooded hills of Oregon are a
backdrop. The 1,200-mile-long Columbia is one
of the largest rivers in the world, draining an
area of 257,000 square miles. I will view its
greatness many more times in my back road
journey through Washington State.

The Columbia River,
Cowlitz County

Old pilings,
Columbia River,
Wahkiakum County

TO CATHLAMET   Taylor Sands Road   ↑ CASTLE ROCK

④

sketch X

2.9
2.8
Willow Grove Road
Willow Grove Rd.
1.7
Mt. Solo Road
Barlow Point Road
Mt. Solo Road
5.5
Columbia River
④
432   LONGVIEW

The map includes the following labels:

4 GRAYS RIVER
SKAMOKAWA
Brooks Slough Road
2.5
Columbian White-Tailed Deer Nat. Wildlife Refuge
Steamboat Slough Road
4.6
Foster Road
no signs
Longstain Road
Nelson Creek Road
Foster Road
1.1
.7
4
1.3
407
.8
Cathlamet Channel
.7
CATHLAMET
LONGVIEW
4
W. Bernie Slough Rd.
Lower Island Dike Road
Crossdike Rd.
Puget Island
Little Island Road
Little Island
Island Road
Schoolhouse Rd.
409
E. Bernie
Welcome Slough Rd.
Sunny Sands West Road
TOLL FERRY TO OREGON

The road along Steamboat Slough

I travel along dike roads past farms and waterways and am struck by the bouquets of wild grass, flowers, and sometimes young trees that grow from the tops of old pilings. Many are quite decorative, as if specially arranged for the delectation of travelers on back roads.

On Puget Island, south of Cathlamet, are other dike roads. A toll ferry from the island crosses the Columbia River into Oregon.

Grays River Covered Bridge road

This trip is through green meadows and forest land with views of Grays River, farms, barns, and cows. The bridge was built in 1905 and is the only covered bridge in Washington still in use by cars. I make my drawing and proceed across it and along a road lined with wild flowers.

Grays River Covered Bridge,
Wahkiakum County

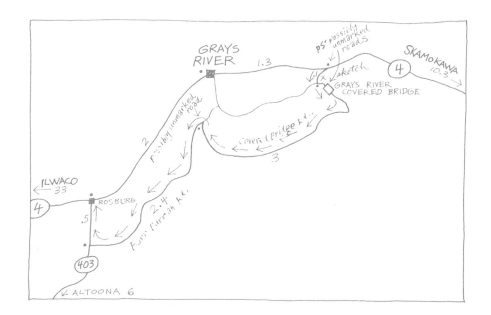

GRAYS RIVER 1.3   PS: possibly unmarked roads

SKAMOKAWA 10.3

(4)

sketch

X

GRAYS RIVER COVERED BRIDGE

2 possibly unmarked road

Covered Bridge Rd.

3

ILWACO ←33

(4)

.5 ROSBURG

2.4 Fern Parrah Rd.

(403)

← ALTOONA 6

Wild blackberry,
Pacific County

Back road to Tsako-te-hahsh-eetl

Foliage here is so dense, at times the road seems walled with green. There are some cranberry bogs, a lovely old hillside cemetery nestled in lush green forest and, at Nahcotta, heaps of Willapa Bay oyster shells. Oysterville, called by Indians Tsako-te-hahsh-eetl (*Land of the Red-top Grass and Home of the Woodpecker*), is a charming hamlet where descendants of the co-founder, R. H. Espy, still live.

In my drawing you see the 1869 W. W. Little house and the Oysterville Church, its orange and white roof topped by a gleaming gold ball. A venerable organ stands on each side of the interior of the church — no doubt producing music as rich as a stereo hi-fi.

An immersion tank below the floor for baptisms, I was told, was used only once, because no drain had been installed.

I observe what I call "hesitation light" in Oysterville. Being near the coast and most often cloudy, the light suddenly brightens or fades, depending upon the intensity of changing cloud layers.

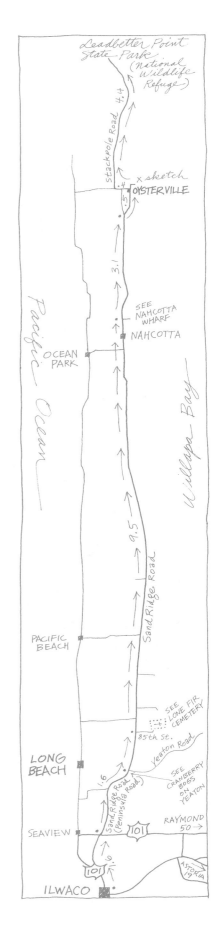

26

Oysterville,
Pacific County

27

The road to Bay Center

Harry Bochau, pronounced Bó-haw, once owned this house in the quiet little fishing and oyster town of Bay Center. I talked to his son, who has since sold it, and learned that the old house had been called "The Château." Harry planted the monkey puzzle tree, a tall Chilean evergreen; I had also seen one at the Hulda Klager lilac gardens. Its intertwined branches and stiff sharp-pointed leaves are a challenge to draw.

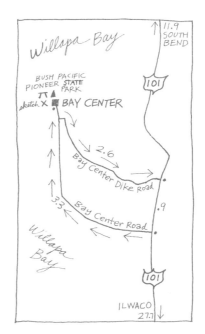

The Château,
Bay Center,
Pacific County

29

A road through Willapa country

This is a rolling, verdant landscape of forest and farms— a country for lumbering and dairies. I sketch the Willow River Dairy with its big 1910 barn and the milk parlor on the left, the old 1889 house, and the railroad bridge.

The owner of the farm bicycles out to meet me while I am sketching. She tells me of the many demanding routines that must be maintained on a dairy farm, in addition to the obvious daily necessity of milking the cows. Later I lunch at a hillside cemetery and take in a grand view of Willapa Valley.

Willow River Dairy, 1889,
Pacific County

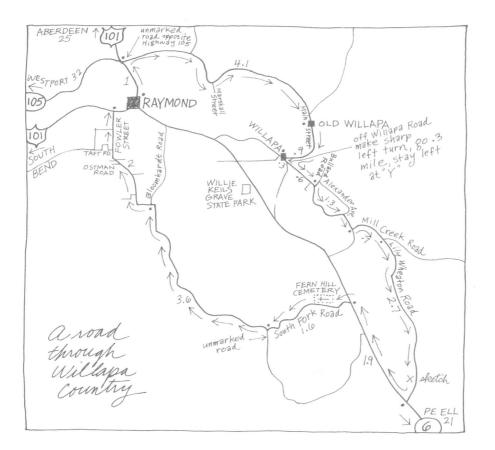

A road through Willapa Country

Rainbow Falls and Boistfort roads

    Scenes along the road from Rainbow Falls State Park include an old covered railroad bridge (now without train rails), forest, farms, and glimpses of the Chehalis River. Past Boistfort the road runs through glorious farm country—meadows green with crops of corn, hay, and peas.
    Wildwood Dairy features a tall, dark blue silo. The young owner left his Dairy Science course at college to run this 170-acre farm.

Chandler Road
3.4
Elk Creek Rd. Stevens Rd.
Kobe Road
→ Leudinghaus Road →
3.4
Meskill Road
Toppelt Rd. 1.1
.8 ⛺ ▲
1.4
3
Stevens Road
← RAINBOW FALLS STATE PARK
Ceres Hill
CHEHALIS 9 →
OLD RAILROAD BRIDGE
(6)
(6)
Ceres Hill Road
3
(ARCHED BRIDGE)
(6)
PE ELL 5.5
WHITE RD.
.2
BOISTFORT RD.
Curtis Hill Road
Moon Hill Road
King Road
7.4 Hubbard Road
McDonald Road
BOISTFORT
PE ELL
14.4
X sketch
CHEHALIS 24
Wildwood Road
RYDERWOOD ↓ (506)

Canada Thistle, Lewis County

33

34

Wildwood Dairy, Lewis County

35

Puyallup Glacier,
Mt. Rainier, Pierce County

36

The back road to see Puyallup
and Tahoma glaciers

There are two confused fawns on
the road, not knowing which way to
go to escape my oncoming vehicle.
They finally bolt off through Douglas
fir, western hemlock, and red cedar
forest, and are soon hidden among
vine maple, moss and fern. At the
viewpoint of Puyallup Glacier, its
river pounds down the mountain with
rock-crushing force, yet on the banks
close by, in all tranquility, grow dainty
columbine, daisies, penstemon, tiger
lily, cow parsnip, lungwort, and other
wild flowers.
The Tahoma Glacier, which I sketch
on the return trip, plays hide-and-seek
with me, great mists and clouds constantly
rearranging themselves on the mountain.
Outsized horseflies circle, keeping up a
constant hum, but they do not bite.
Majestic Mount Rainier with its 27
glaciers and 14,410-foot height is stunning
and awe-inspiring—what a mountain!

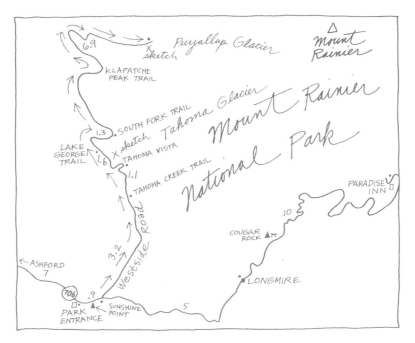

Tahoma Glacier,
Mt. Rainier,
Pierce County

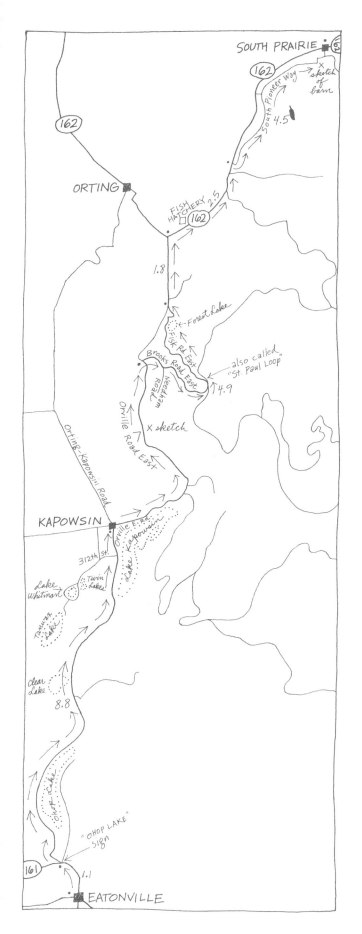

Back road from Eatonville

The road passes Ohop
Lake through the lush meadow
and farm landscape of Ohop
Valley to Kopowsin Lake
and South Prairie town.
I stop along the way at
the fish hatchery to watch
tiny salmon leaping about.
One leaps too far!
It jumps onto a gravel
path and I return it to the
water. Near South Prairie
I draw the Winters barn.
Mrs. Winters tells people
who look for the farm,
"watch for the ugliest barn!"
I equip myself with a
can of dog repellent, which
Mrs. Winters gives to me in
case the big ram should come
close and lower his head in
my direction. "Don't turn
your back on him," she
cautions. The formidable
ram chews a bit on my
folding chair while I sit
in the meadow and sketch,
but luckily that is all.

Seen on the road to South Prairie, Pierce County

Winters Barn,
near South Prairie, Pierce County

The road to Wilkeson and Mowich Lake

The early settlers of Wilkeson, a town rimmed by conifer forest, were the immigrants who worked in local coal mines. Mining declined in the area around 1912, but in 1883 the nearby Carbonado mines were the second largest in Washington. The nicely restored Orthodox church, topped with a pale blue onion dome, is the oldest of its kind in Washington. It is located on Long Street. If you drive north to Short Street, then east to Cothery Street, you will see a castle.

Holy Trinity Orthodox Church, 1900,
Wilkeson, Pierce County

44

It was constructed by a Wilkeson carpenter who dreamed of building and living in his own castle. The owner isn't home when I visit, but I talk to his neighbor through a screen door as he watches television. "I don't mind a castle going up next door," he comments in good cheer.

I then drive to glacially formed Mowich Lake, which is surrounded by high-ridged peaks and trails that invite investigation.

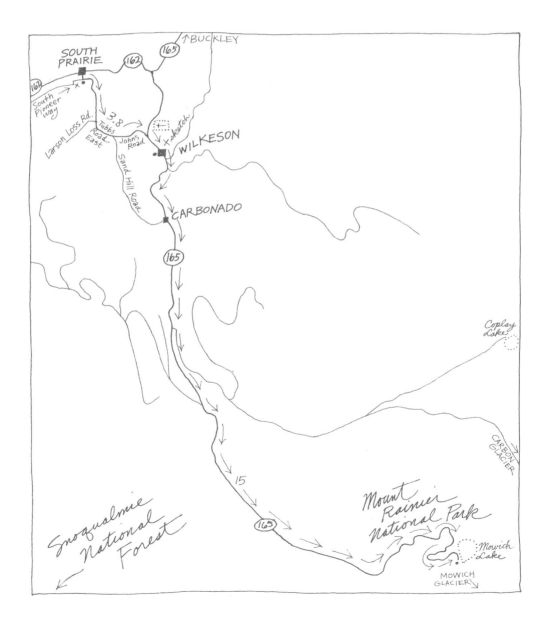

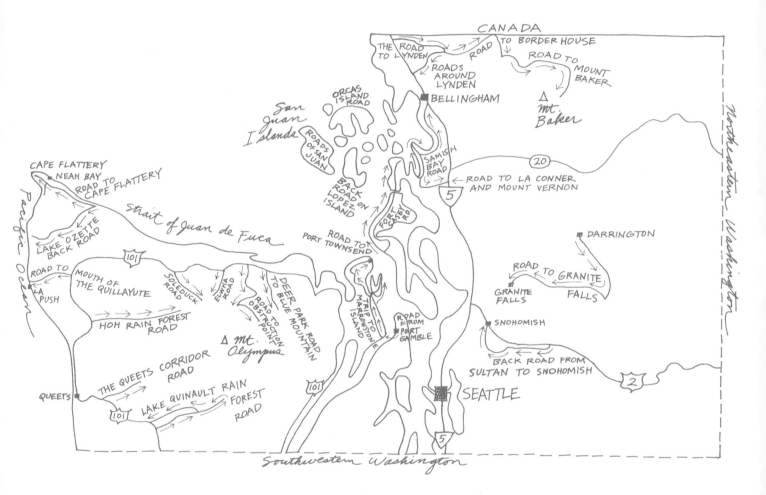

Northwestern Washington

I recall the rich greenness of the Olympic forest, the Alpine glory of Mount Olympus, a view of Tatoosh Island off Cape Flattery bathed in sunshine, the fun of ferryboat rides among the San Juans, the neatly arranged farms of the descendants of the early Dutch settlers near Lynden, and uncooperative Mount Baker that would not come out of its cloud cover so I could draw it.

Fireweed,
Snohomish County

Lake Quinault rain forest road

Hemlock, alder, cedar, maple, and fir
are all draped with moss. Soft light
filters to a forest floor blanketed
with fern and oxalis. I ride on a good
gravel road that is narrow in spots
and has obviously been planned with
the beauty of the landscape in mind
rather than speed. At the end of the
road foot trails begin beside clear,
rushing Grave Creek.

Forest road,
Olympic National Park,
Grays Harbor and Jefferson Counties

49

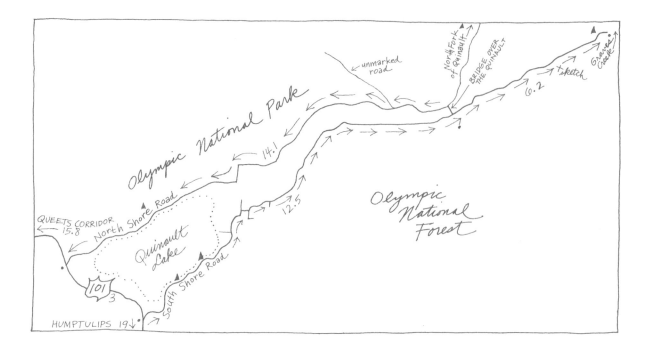

Olympic National Park

unmarked road

North Fork of Quinault

BRIDGE OVER THE QUINAULT

0.2   sketch   Graves Creek

Olympic National Forest

14.1

12.5

North Shore Road

QUEETS CORRIDOR 15.8

Quinault Lake

South Shore Road

101   3

HUMPTULIPS 19

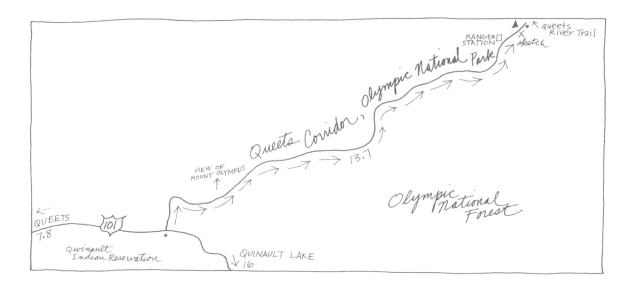

RANGER STATION   X   sketch   queets River Trail

Queets Corridor, Olympic National Park

VIEW OF MOUNT OLYMPUS   13.7

Olympic National Forest

QUEETS 7.8   101

Quinault Indian Reservation

QUINAULT LAKE 16

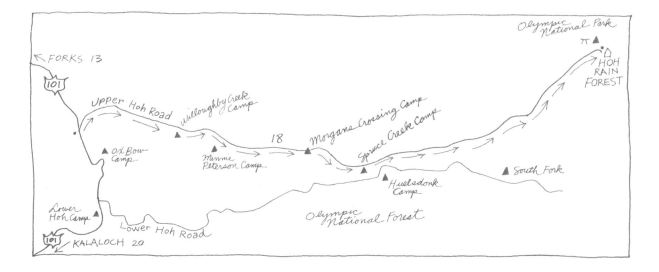

Olympic National Park

FORKS 13

101

HOH RAIN FOREST

Upper Hoh Road   Willoughby Creek Camp

Morgans Crossing Camp

18   Spruce Creek Camp

Ox Bow Camp

Minnie Peterson Camp

Huelsdonk Camp

South Fork

Lower Hoh Camp

Lower Hoh Road

Olympic National Forest

101   KALALOCH 20

The Queets Corridor road

The road following Queets River runs through a deep rain forest. At the end of the corridor I have a fine view of the Queets. A sign at the beginning of a hike from here states, "You must ford the Queets River first before taking the trail.

It is wide and rocky and you must choose a good spot since it changes from year to year. After a rainfall it might be too difficult to ford."

Trails go up the Queets River or branch off along Tshletshy Creek to the North Fork of the Quinault River.

The road to Hoh Rain Forest is another that must be experienced. At Hoh there are short walks one can take to see epiphytes (air plants) in profusion and thick draperies of club moss, giant Sitka spruce, hemlock, fir, red cedar, and red alder. All this green glory is supported by about 142 inches of rain each year in the Hoh Valley.

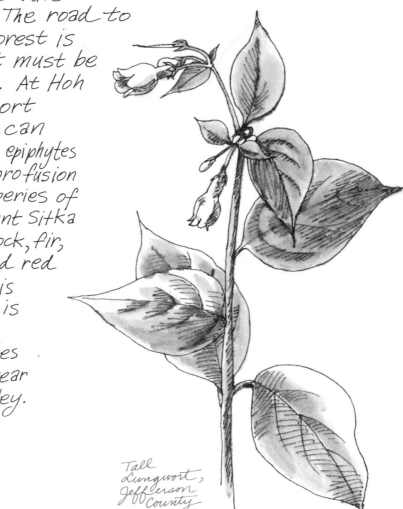

Tall Lungwort, Jefferson County

Rain forest,
Queets Corridor,
Jefferson County

53

at the mouth
of the Quillayute River

The road to the mouth of the Quillayute

It is a fast back road through the forest to the beach opposite La Push at the mouth of the Quillayute. The village looks inviting from the Rialto Beach side, near Mora. Once there, however, it isn't quite as picturesque, although the fishing boats and wharf activity lend some excitement to the town. I sketch James Island across the Quillayute and a fishing boat bringing in its catch.

Mora Beach has naturalist walks and trails leading to other beaches, which are separated by bold, rocky headlands.

Ozette Lake back road

No road at all reached Ozette until about 1930. The Scandinavians who homesteaded the area had to pack in along the Hoko River trail. Now the road follows the Hoko River and Big River to tranquil Ozette Lake. Here trail heads begin to Sand Point and to Cape Alava. Excavations were made just north of the cape in the early 1980s where an Ozette Indian village was buried by mud some four hundred years ago.

Ozette Lake, Clallam County

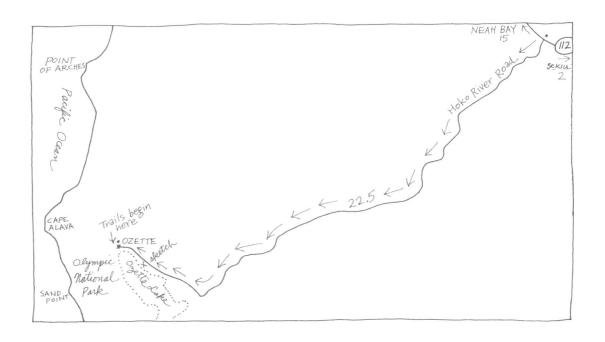

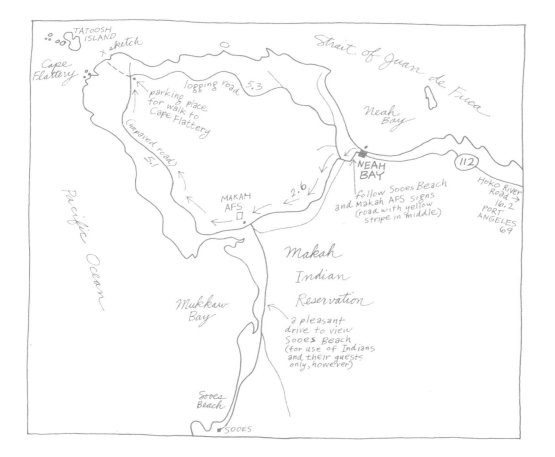

TATOOSH
ISLAND
× sketch

Cape
Flattery

parking
place
for walk to
Cape Flattery

logging road   5.3

(unpaved road)
5.1

MAKAH
AFS

2.6

Strait of Juan de Fuca

Neah
Bay

NEAH
BAY

112

follow Sooes Beach
and Makah AFS signs
(road with yellow
stripe in middle)

Hoko River
Road
16.2
PORT
ANGELES
69

Pacific Ocean

Makah

Indian

Reservation

a pleasant
drive to view
Sooes Beach
(for use of Indians
and their guests
only, however)

Mukkaw
Bay

Sooes
Beach

SOOES

The road to Cape Flattery

It is foggy along the Strait of
Juan de Fuca, so I am surprised and pleased
to find Cape Flattery in bright sunshine. The
trail to the dramatic viewpoint is a root-strewn
path. The roots spread out from the base of
ancient red cedars and sitka spruce. Scores
of boats pass by, including a black-hulled
sailing ship. A young bald eagle pursued by seabirds
flies to cover in the forest. Feeling a part of
all the drama, I sketch the island from a
cliffside perch, as Tatoosh's lighthouse horn
booms a mournful cry across the
sunlit sea.

Tatoosh Island,
Cape Flattery,
Clallam County

The road to Obstruction Point

The road to Soleduck, the road along the Elwha River, and the road to Hurricane Ridge are beautiful trips and easily driven. The road to Obstruction Point, which takes off from Hurricane Ridge, is bumpy and steep at times. There are astonishing vistas to enjoy, including an expansive view of Puget Sound with snow-capped Mount Baker on the horizon.

Alpine flowers carpet the hillsides and sub-Alpine fir make spiky vignettes on the slopes where I sketch some of the glacier-carved peaks of Olympic National Park. Competitors in a footrace, which began at Deer Park, run past and greet me with a smile and wave of the hand.

Avalanche Lily, Clallam County

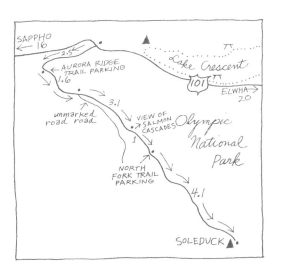

SAPPHO ←16

2.5

← AURORA RIDGE
TRAIL PARKING
1.6

unmarked
road road

3.1

VIEW OF
SALMON
CASCADES

Olympic
National
Park

1

NORTH
FORK TRAIL
PARKING

Lake Crescent

101

ELWHA →
20

4.1

SOLEDUCK ▲

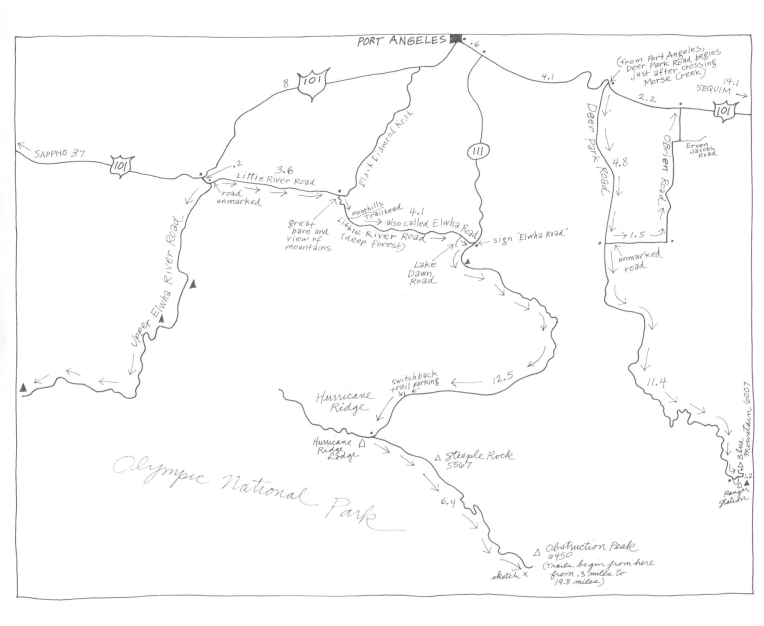

PORT ANGELES ■ .6

8 101

4.1

(from Port Angeles,
Deer Park Road begins
just after crossing
Morse Creek)

14.1
SEQUIM →

101

2.2

SAPPHO 37

101

.2
Little River Road
3.6

road
unmarked

Black Diamond Road

111

Deer Park Road

O'Brien Road

Erven
Jacobs
Road

4.8

Foothills
Trailhead
Little River Road
(deep forest)

4.1
also called Elwha Road

great
barn and
view of
mountains

sign "Elwha Road"

1.5

unmarked
road

Lake
Dawn
Road

▲

Upper Elwha River Road

11.4

switchback
trail parking

12.5

Hurricane
Ridge

Hurricane
Ridge
Lodge △

△ Steeple Rock
5567

Blue Mountain 6007

1.2

▲
Ranger
Station

Olympic National Park

6.4

△ Obstruction Peak
6450
(Trails begin from here
from .3 miles to
19.8 miles)

sketch X

Mt. Olympus
from Obstruction Point,
Clallam County

Piper Bell,
found only in
Olympic
National Park

Bush
Cinquefoil,
Blue Mountain,
Olympic National
Park

Deer Park Road to Blue Mountain

The sharp, upthrust peaks of the Olympic Range are some 70 million years old but, geologically, they are considered new mountains. The serious exploration of the Olympics began in 1889 when James Christie, financed by a Seattle newspaper, led a trip into the mountains.

From time to time the passing of oncoming vehicles requires great caution on the narrow road toward the top of Blue Mountain. At the crest, on that pleasant clear day, I let time slip away and forget my own concerns, as I look out on the spaciousness of nature. In their rock crevice habitat I sketch buttery yellow cinquefoil and pale lavender piper bell, found only in Olympic National Park.

Lowbush Penstemon,
Clallam County

The road from Port Gamble

Port Gamble, a historic mill town on a bluff overlooking the Hood Canal, was built by settlers to resemble their beloved East Machias, Maine. Saint Paul's Episcopal Church, 1870, was modeled after the Congregational Church of East Machias.

The steeple bell arrived by sailing vessel in 1879 and still calls people to worship on Sundays. I enjoy reading sentimental epitaphs in the shaded graveyard overlooking the canal.

One reads, "Shed not for her the bitter tear / Nor give the heart to vain regret / Tis but the casket that lies here / The gem that filled it sparkles yet."

St. Paul's Church,
Port Gamble,
Kitsap County

If you stay off Hwy.20 and go straight, the road comes out on 19th Street. Go right on Walker Street and left on Washington street.

follow Monroe, Roosevelt and Jackson Sts. to Fort

Fort Worden State Park.

Admiralty Inlet

Cape George

4.8

unmarked road

x sketch

PORT TOWNSEND

Mystery Bay

Beckett Point

20

2.8

Discovery Bay

1.1

.3

Discovery Bay to left

Indian Island

Fort Flagler State Park

sketch

2.9

County Road 12

.3

1.9

IRONDALE

Marrowstone Island

County Road 18

.8

2.7

NORDLAND

Jefferson County Park

1.4

East Marrowstone Road
Robbins Rd.

Puget Sound

8.3

PORT LUDLOW

104

2.9

Ludlow Paradise Road

3

104
Shine Rd.

W.R.Hicks County Park

2.

PORT GAMBLE

sketch

SOUTH POINT

Hood Canal

104

3

104

The old lighthouse, Marrowstone Island, Jefferson County

A trip to Marrowstone Island

In 1792 Captain George Vancouver
of the Royal British Navy charted the
entrance to Puget Sound and found that
the high bluffs of the island there looked
as if they were composed of marrow stone.
(The island was named after this material.)
Fort Flagler State Park is situated on the
north end of the island and, while there, I
draw a view of the 1895 lighthouse, Puget
Sound, and Mount Baker. Many of the
original buildings of Fort Flagler, founded
in 1887, are still standing and are
part of the fascination of
Marrowstone Island.

Road to Port Townsend

There is a sign, hand-painted by the ranger, at Rothschild House in Port Townsend. It says, "111 YEARS OLD. MOST ITEMS ORIGINAL. ENTRY WALL-PAPER—1891, PARLOR—1885. YOUNGEST DAUGHTER LIVED HERE 78 YEARS, LAST 36 ALONE. MR. R. OWNED GEN. STORE DOWN TOWN. 5 CHILDREN, 3 GRAND. YOUNGEST SON GAVE HOUSE TO STATE PARKS IN 1958. A NICE FAMILY MEMORIAL!"

Port Townsend was named by Captain George Vancouver in 1792 in honor of the Marquis of Townshend. It has many buildings and houses of historic interest and is picturesquely situated on a bluff overlooking the bay and Admiralty Inlet.

Fort Worden State Park nearby, with its fort buildings and old lighthouse, is also quite interesting.

Henry's original stove, Rothschild House, Port Townsend, Jefferson County

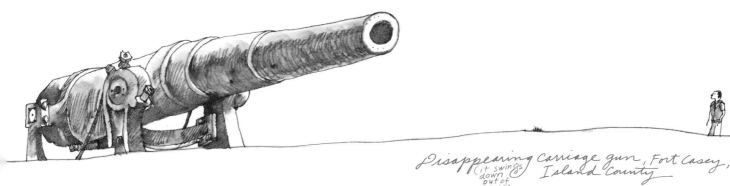

Disappearing carriage gun, Fort Casey,
Island County
(it swings
down
out of
sight)

Fort Casey to Coupeville and Oak Harbor

Big gun emplacements overlook Admiralty Inlet and point at passing ships. While I sketch, a work party of young people are painting the guns, which glisten in their new olive gray coat. The old lighthouse is now a display center, with photographs and historical material.

There are three state parks on Whidbey Island: Fort Casey, South Whidbey, and Deception Pass.

If you pick up an Island County map you may investigate all the roads on quiet, agricultural Whidbey Island.

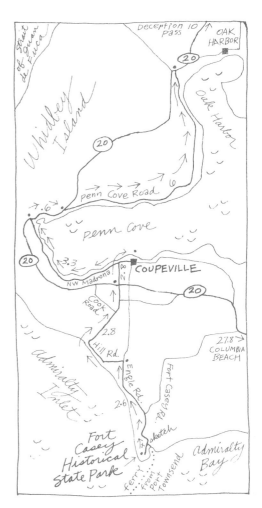

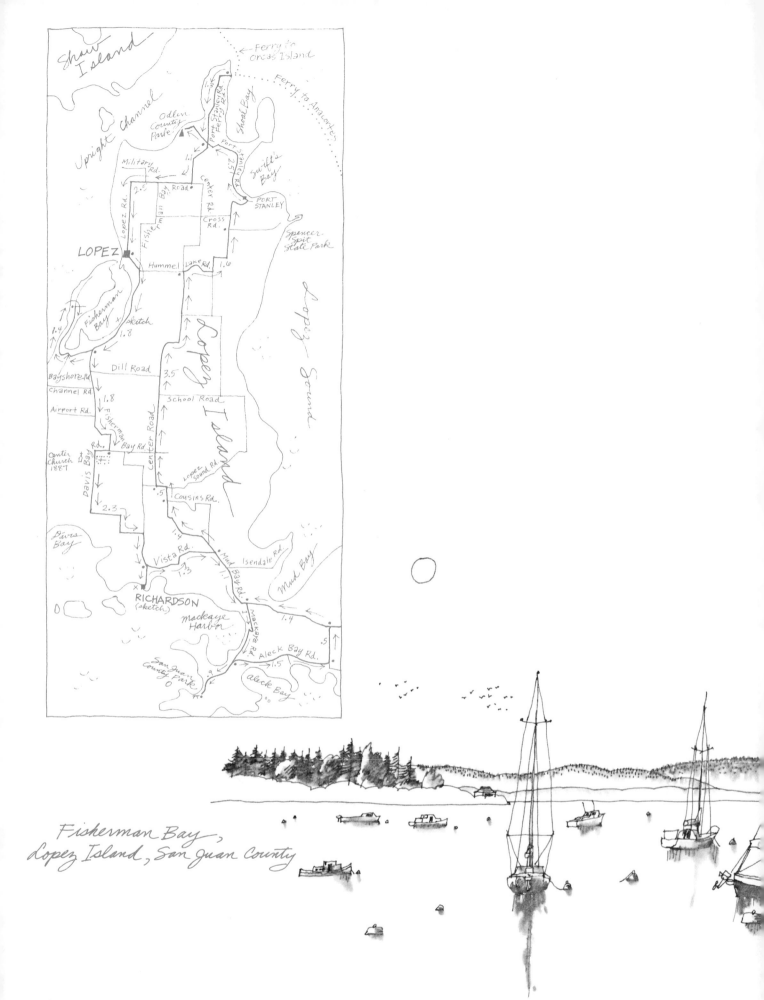

Shaw Island

Ferry to Orcas Island

Ferry to Anacortes

Upright Channel

Odlin County Park

1.1

Port Stanley Ferry Rd.

Shoal Bay

Military Rd.

2.5

Fisherman Bay Road

Center Rd.

2.5

Port Stanley Rd.

Swift's Bay

Lopez Rd.

1.1

PORT STANLEY

LOPEZ

Cross Rd.

Spencer Spit State Park

Hummel Lake Rd.   1.6

Fisherman Bay

x sketch

1.4   1.8

Lopez Sound

Bayshore Rd.

Dill Road   3.5

Lopez Island

Channel Rd.

1.8

School Road

Airport Rd.

Fisherman Bay Rd.

Center Road

Center Church 1887

Davis Bay Rd.

Lopez Sound Rd.

2.3

.5   Cousins Rd.

Davis Bay

1.4

Vista Rd.

Isendale Rd.

Mud Bay Rd.

Mud Bay

1.1

1.3

RICHARDSON
(sketch)

Mackaye Harbor

.1   1.4

.1   Mackaye Rd.

.5

San Juan County Park

.9   Aleck Bay Rd.

1.5

Aleck Bay

Fisherman Bay,
Lopez Island, San Juan County

Back road on Lopez Island

It is incredibly calm at Fisherman Bay in the early morning. Motorboats have not started up as yet and the cries of seabirds resound across the water.

At Richardson I sketched the General Store. Before it burned down on October 27, 1990, it was a friendly place, its shelves and tables laden with groceries, dry goods, sundries and hardware. The village was settled by George Richardson, who established a farm there about 1870. A lively fishing port around 1900, it is now again a quiet and serene village.

Richardson General Store,
Lopez Island, San Juan County

Orcas Island Road

On the way to Orcas Island the ferry stops at the charming, well-tended, flower-bedecked dock at Shaw Island. Nuns are arriving to open the little chapel on the pier. This island, although quite lovely, seems somewhat private, and I continue on to Orcas.

Orcas is the largest of the 172 islands that comprise the archipelago of the San Juans. I drive to the top of the 2,400-foot Mount Constitution for views of the islands and mainland beyond. A sign from the 1890s declares this to be "the finest marine view in all of North America." A stone tower at the top, built in the 1930s, was patterned after 12th-century European watchtowers.

Its architect had this message engraved in metal at the site: "To him who restores, my sincere commendation. To one who would alter, eternal damnation." Ellsworth Storey, 1936.

Orcas Island ferry, San Juan County

President Channel

West Beach

West Beach Rd

West Beach Rd .3

2.4 1.3

.5 EASTSOUND

East Sound

Oros to Olga Road

4.

△ Mt. Constitution 2409

4.8

Mountain Lake

1.4

Cascade Lake

1.4

ROSARIO RESORT

Island

Olga and Doe Bay Road

Doe Bay

Olga to Kl Lawrence Road

Rosario Strait

Orcas

OLGA

4.3

Deer Harbor Road

4

DEER HARBOR

.9

West Sound

Horseshoe Hwy.

2.6

ORCAS

Ferry to Friday Harbor

Ferry to Lopez

Shaw Island

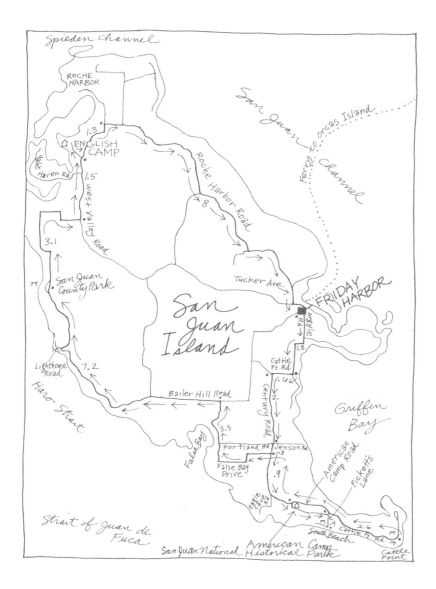

Spieden Channel

ROCHE HARBOR

San Juan to Orcas Island

Ferry to Orcas Channel

1.3

ENGLISH CAMP

West Valley Haven Rd

1.5

West Valley Road

Roche Harbor Road

.8

3.1

San Juan County Park

Tucker Ave.

FRIDAY HARBOR

San Juan Island

Argyle Rd

1.8

Cattle Pt. Rd.

.6

Lighthouse Road

7.2

Bailer Hill Road

Haro Strait

Century Road

.2

Griffin Bay

3.3

False Bay

Portland Rd.

Jenson Rd

1.3

False Bay Drive

.9

American Camp Road

Pickett's Lane

Eagle Cove Rd.

Strait of Juan de Fuca

.4

Cattle Pt. Rd.

2.6

South Beach

San Juan National

American Camp Historical Park

Cattle Point

English Camp, San Juan Island,
San Juan County.

Roads of San Juan

At the National Park on the road around the island there is a historical display. At South Beach the shore is long and strewn with water-worn logs. Farther on is a good view of False Bay with the Olympic mountain range in the background. With the tide out, there are plenty of tide pools to inspect.

At English Camp I sketch the blockhouse built around 1860 when the old fort was in its heyday. The British flag is still flown here, respecting the peaceful settlement of a border dispute in which they declared the San Juan Islands to be American rather than Canadian land. There is a grove of magnificent maple trees nearby, and the ranger tells me that one tree that has been core-tested is over three hundred years old.

Road to La Conner and Mount Vernon

Colorful flower baskets ornament stores along
the main street of the fishing village of La Conner.
I sketch the town from across the Swinomish Channel.
Gaches Mansion, a twenty-two-room historic house on
Second Street, is at top left in the picture, and a
big blue-and-white sockeye salmon purse seiner
boat is in the foreground.

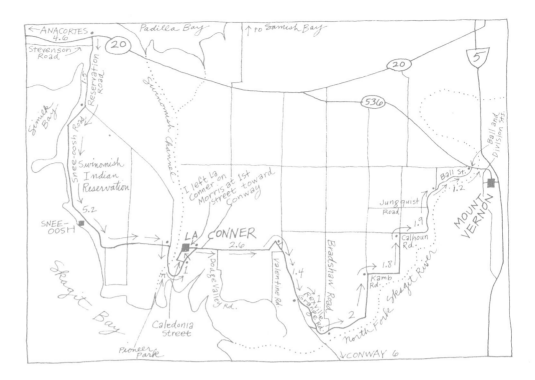

A Swinomish Indian boy, who watches me draw, tells me proudly that he has an eighteen-foot boat with which he fishes for king salmon. Just then a large pleasure boat passes with an auxiliary boat perched on it. "Lotsa cash for that," he says, "the boat on the stern is as big as mine."

The purse seiner is being readied for sea and, before I finish my drawing, its crew waves good-bye to relatives ashore as it sails away.

Sockeye Purse Seiner,
La Conner, Skagit County

Samish Bay,
Skagit County

82

Samish Bay road

A steep wooden
stairway goes to Samish
Island Public Beach, which
offers fifteen hundred
feet of tideland for
people's use. The bay is
a spawning ground for
the Pacific oyster, and
intertidal hardshell clams
and Dungeness crabs can
be found at the beach
at low tide.

This beach of rocks and barnacles is a most
tranquil place. There is the faint hum of commerce
in the distance, but the cries of seabirds fill
the air. A great blue heron flies by and I can
hear the air rush through its wings.

The road to Lynden

The Peace Arch in Blaine commemorates the hundred years of open border shared by Canada and the United States between 1814 and 1914. After visiting the arch and its gardens, I drive through green, rolling meadowlands to Lynden. At Hans C. Berthusen Park, an ideal picnic spot, I draw the red barn shown on the next page with its bold white markings. Hans and Lida's old stump privy stands to the right of the barn. On the left is a 1906 threshing machine. Old tractors and antique farm machinery are arriving for Lynden's annual threshing bee and each engine makes its own "pock pock" sound. I sketch a McCormick-Deering W61 tractor from the thirties, nicknamed "The Outhouse" after its box like homemade cab.

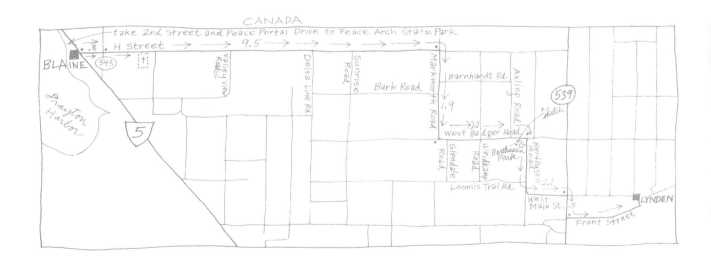

"The Outhouse",
Lynden, Whatcom County

Berthusen Barn, Lynden, Whatcom County

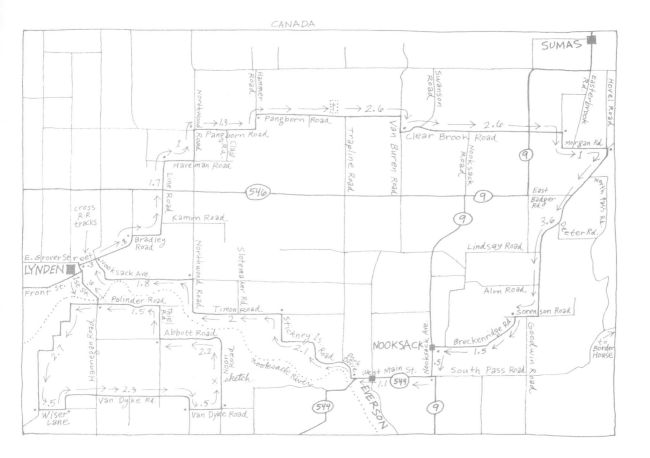

CANADA

SUMAS

Hammer Road
Northwood Road
Pangborn Road
1.3
Pangborn Road
1
Clay Rd.
Haveman Road
1.7
Line Road
546
Trapline Road
Van Buren Road
Swanson Road
Clear Brook Road
2.6
2.6
Nooksack Road
9
1
Morgan Rd.
Easterbrook Rd.
Hovel Road
9
East Badger Rd.
3.6
Deeter Rd.
North Pass Rd.

cross
R.R.
tracks
Kamm Road
.8
Bradley Road
E. Grover Street
LYNDEN
Nooksack Ave.
.3
.6
1st St.
Front St.
Polinder Road
1.5
Hannegan Road
2.7
.5
Wiser Lane
Van Dyke Rd.
2.3
Northwood Road
Slotemaker Rd.
1.8
Thiel Rd.
Timon Road
2
Abbott Road
2.2
Noon Road
Nooksack River
decon sketch
Stickney Is. Road
2.1
Park
.5
Van Dyke Road
Lindsay Road
Alm Road
Sorenson Road
Breckenridge Rd.
1.5
Goodwin Road
to Border House
NOOKSACK
Nooksack Ave.
.5
South Pass Road
West Main St.
1.1
544
EVERSON
544
9

88

The Dutch heritage of Lynden's settlers is reflected in the tidy character of its homes and farms. The neatness is enhanced by rows of flowers in gardens and window boxes. Big, handsome barns dot the green landscape. I sketch the graceful yellow-and-white Dykstra brothers' 1930s milking barn, which towers over the original barn. The new metal milking barn (not as picturesque) is to the left, out of my picture.

DE
DYKSTRA
BOERDERIJ

The Dykstra brothers' Barn, Whatcom County

The road to Border House

This route touches the Canadian border, although no legal road continues from here into Canada. Border House once stood here with many a whimsical display for the enjoyment of visitors. The house burned down, however, in the late 1980s.

The wagon and milk cans in my drawing were painted red, white and blue. All the birds pictured were alive except the owl. The quaint, Greek Revival-style house included a room where Teddy Roosevelt is supposed to have spent the night.

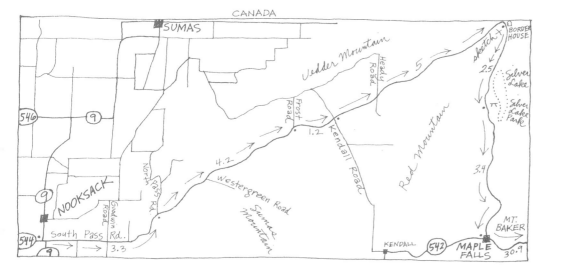

Sign at Border House, Whatcom County

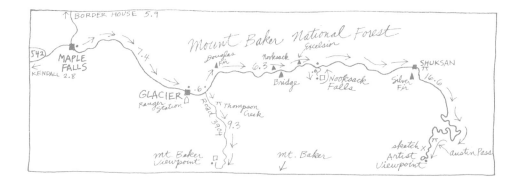

Mount Baker National Forest

↑ BORDER HOUSE 5.9
542
MAPLE FALLS
← KENDALL 2.8
7.4
Douglas Fir
Nooksack
Excelsior
6.3
Bridge
Nooksack Falls
SHUKSAN 16.6
Silver Fir
GLACIER
Ranger Station
.6
Road 3904
π Thompson Creek
9.3
mt. Baker Viewpoint
mt. Baker
sketch Artist Viewpoint
austin Pass

The road to Mount Baker

A wet gravel road banked with snow leads to Artist Point, which is supposed to provide a good view of Mount Baker. Once there, I am enveloped in thick, misty clouds and only occasionally does a break appear in the rolling fogbanks. I decide not to go away empty-handed, however, so here you see a drawing of the foreground. You must drive to Artist Point to put mighty Mount Baker in the background and complete my picture!

Timber line,
Mt. Baker,
Whatcom county

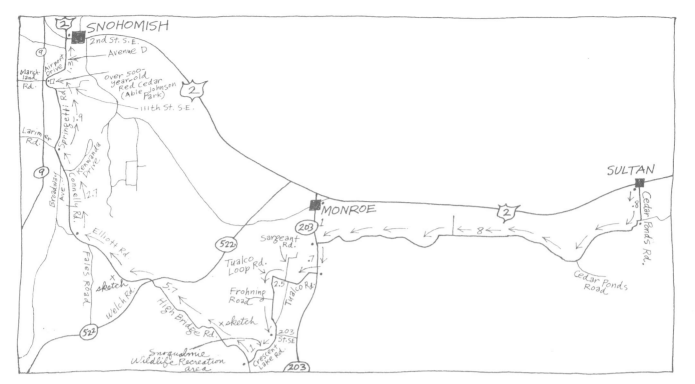

Back road from Sultan to Snohomish

The road from Sultan follows the
Skykomish River. From Tualco Road the
scenery is green and hilly with
dairy-country barns and
farmhouses silhouetted against
forest backgrounds. Along the
way I sketch a small milking
barn that has been fashioned into
a house. At Ricville farm I
draw a landscape encompassing
most of the farm's buildings
and some of the Holstein herd.

milking barn-house,
near Monroe,
Snohomish County

Snohomish County farm

Tom Thumb Grocery,
Granite Falls,
Snohomish County

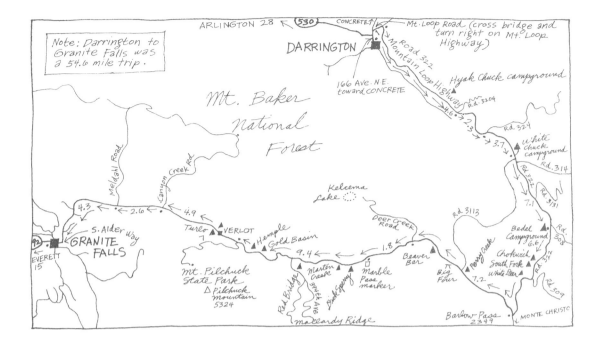

Note: Darrington to Granite Falls was a 54.6 mile trip.

ARLINGTON 28 ← 530 CONCRETE↑
DARRINGTON
Mt. Loop Road (cross bridge and turn right on Mt. Loop Highway)
166 Ave. N.E. toward CONCRETE
Road 322
Mountain Loop Highway
Hyak Chuck campground
Rd. 3204
Rd 324
4.6
2.3
3.7
White Chuck campground
Rd. 314
Mt. Baker National Forest
Meldahl Road
Canyon Creek Rd.
Kelcema Lake
Deer Creek Road
Rd. 3113
Rd. 321
Rd 3131
7.1
Bedel Campground
Rd. 308
4.3
2.6
4.9
Turlo
VERLOT
Hemple
Gold Basin
9.4
1.8
Beaver Bar
Perry Creek
6.6
Chokwich South Fork White Bear
Rd. 322
92
GRANITE FALLS
S. Alder Way
mt. Pilchuck State Park
△ Pilchuck Mountain 5324
Red Bridge
Marten Creek
South Ave
Buck Spring
Marble Pass marker
Big Four
7.2
Rd. 509
EVERETT 15
Mallardy Ridge
Barlow Pass 2349
MONTE CHRISTO

Road to Granite Falls

From the lumber town of Darrington, this back road wanders through Mount Baker National Forest. Hemlock, big-leaf maple, vine maple, and alder flourish here. The trunks of the older white alder trees are spotted with green moss. When growing in profusion, they create incredibly intricate patterns in the forest. At Granite Falls I enjoy visiting the busy Tom Thumb Grocery and sketching its aging facade.

Self-Heal (purple flowers), Snohomish County

99

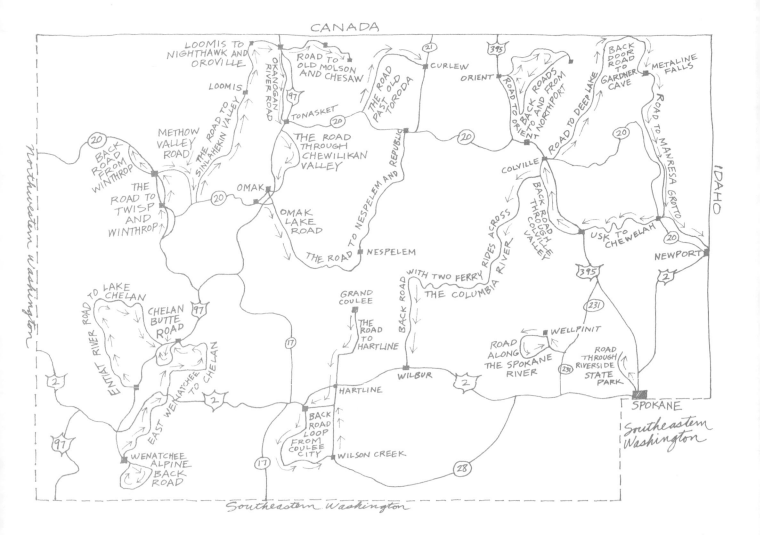

CANADA

LOOMIS TO
NIGHTHAWK AND
OROVILLE

ROAD TO
OLD MOLSON
AND CHESAW

21

395

BACK
DOOR
ROAD
TO
GARDNER
CAVE

METALINE
FALLS

LOOMIS

CURLEW

ORIENT

OKANOGAN RIVER ROAD

97

TONASKET

20

THE ROAD PAST OLD TORODA

20

ROAD TO ORIENT

BACK ROADS INTO AND FROM NORTHPORT

ROAD TO DEEP LAKE

20

ROAD TO MANRESA GROTTO

METHOW
VALLEY
ROAD

THE ROAD TO SINLAHEKIN VALLEY

THE ROAD
THROUGH
CHEWILIKAN
VALLEY

20

BACK
ROAD
FROM
WINTHROP

THE
ROAD TO
TWISP
AND
WINTHROP

20

OMAK

COLVILLE

BACK ROAD THROUGH COLVILLE VALLEY

USK TO CHEWELAH

20

OMAK
LAKE
ROAD

THE ROAD TO NESPELEM AND REPUBLIC

NEWPORT

2

THE ROAD   NESPELEM

395

BACK ROAD WITH TWO FERRY RIDES ACROSS THE COLUMBIA RIVER

231

ROAD TO LAKE CHELAN

CHELAN
BUTTE
ROAD

97

GRAND
COULEE

THE
ROAD
TO
HARTLINE

ROAD
ALONG
THE SPOKANE
RIVER

WELLPINIT

ROAD
THROUGH
RIVERSIDE
STATE
PARK

ENTIAT RIVER ROAD

17

231

2

EAST WENATCHEE TO CHELAN

2

WILBUR

2

SPOKANE

97

HARTLINE

Southeastern Washington

WENATCHEE
ALPINE
BACK
ROAD

BACK
ROAD
LOOP
FROM
COULEE
CITY

WILSON CREEK

17

28

Northeastern Washington

IDAHO

Northeastern Washington

I remember the broad glacially formed valleys and their majestic rivers, the Methow, Okanogan, Similkameen, Kettle, Sanpoil, Pend Oreille, the great Columbia, and others.

I recall orchards bulging with apples; the deep forests of pine, fir, and larch; the lakes of silver hue; and vast wheat fields awaiting harvest, all this along the intriguing back roads of northeastern Washington.

Pearly Everlasting
(white flowers),
Chelan County

Washington apples,
Chelan county

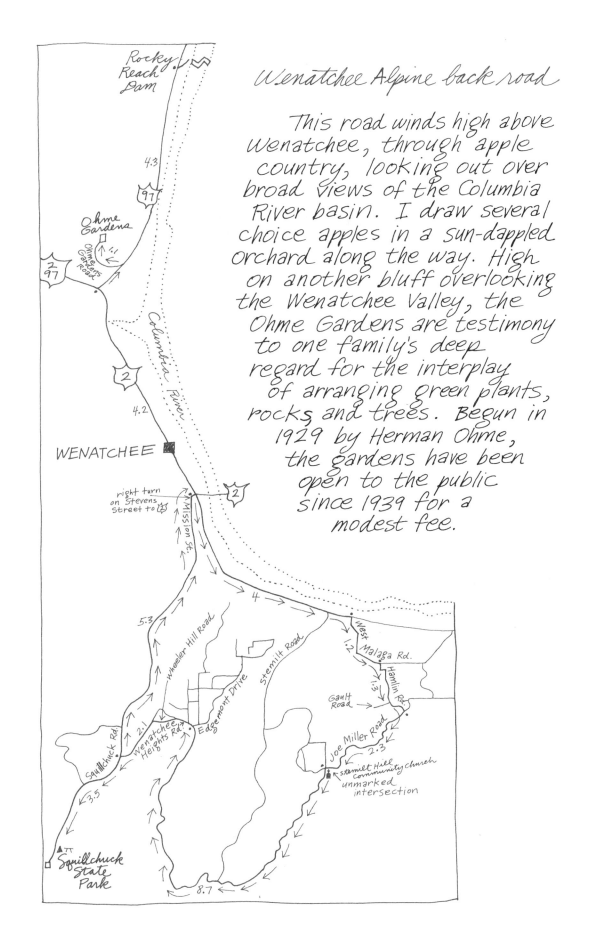

Wenatchee Alpine back road

This road winds high above Wenatchee, through apple country, looking out over broad views of the Columbia River basin. I draw several choice apples in a sun-dappled orchard along the way. High on another bluff overlooking the Wenatchee Valley, the Ohme Gardens are testimony to one family's deep regard for the interplay of arranging green plants, rocks, and trees. Begun in 1929 by Herman Ohme, the gardens have been open to the public since 1939 for a modest fee.

Rocky Reach Dam

4.3

97

Ohme Gardens

Ohme's Garden Road

2 97

2

Columbia River

4.2

WENATCHEE

right turn on Stevens Street to (2)

Mission St.

2

5.3

Wheeler Hill Road

4

West Malaga Rd.

1.2

Stemilt Road

Hamlin Rd.

1.3

Gault Road

Squillchuck Rd.

2.1

Wenatchee Heights Rd.

Edgemont Drive

Joe Miller Road

2.3

3.5

Stemilt Hill Community church
unmarked intersection

Squillchuck State Park

8.7

Log interior,
St. Andrews Church,
Chelan, Chelan County

104

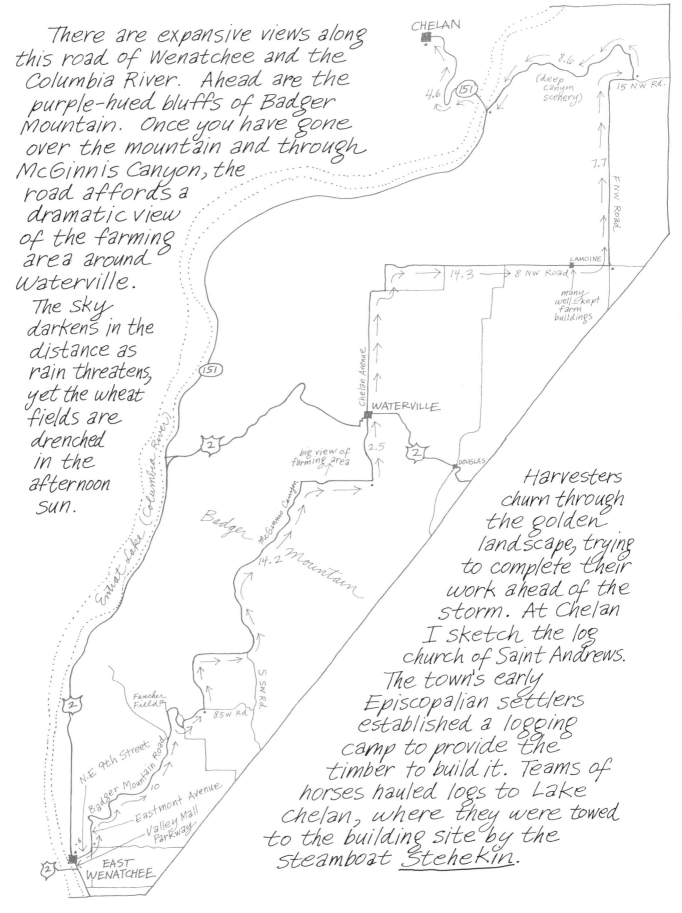

There are expansive views along this road of Wenatchee and the Columbia River. Ahead are the purple-hued bluffs of Badger Mountain. Once you have gone over the mountain and through McGinnis Canyon, the road affords a dramatic view of the farming area around Waterville.

The sky darkens in the distance as rain threatens, yet the wheat fields are drenched in the afternoon sun.

CHELAN

8.6

(deep canyon scenery)

15 NW Rd.

4.6

151

7.7

F NW Road

LAMOINE

14.3 → 8 NW Road

many well kept farm buildings

Chelan Avenue

WATERVILLE

2.5

2

2

DOUGLAS

big view of farming area

Badger

McGinnis Canyon

14.2

Mountain

Entiat Lake (Columbia River)

151

S SW Rd.

Fancher Field

85 W Rd.

N.E 9th Street

Badger Mountain Road

10

Eastmont Avenue

Valley Mall Parkway

.6

2

EAST WENATCHEE

Harvesters churn through the golden landscape, trying to complete their work ahead of the storm. At Chelan I sketch the log church of Saint Andrews. The town's early Episcopalian settlers established a logging camp to provide the timber to build it. Teams of horses hauled logs to Lake Chelan, where they were towed to the building site by the steamboat _Stehekin_.

View of Columbia River from Chelan Butte, Chelan County

Chelan Butte Road

Very soon this road offers a grand view of the Lake Chelan region. It is a narrow dirt road and slow going at times; however, the vistas from Chelan Butte lookout tower are well worth the trip. Colorful hang gliders take off from the slope below the tower, one glider circling up and up until it is only a speck in the sky. My fingers tingle as I watch this extraordinary performance, and I feel particular pleasure in having both feet securely planted upon the earth. With the Cascades as a backdrop, I continue on a primitive but picturesque road that winds past rolling fields of grain and the Columbia River shimmering in sunshine.

Entiat River Road to Chelan

Peach, pear, and apple orchards decorate the banks a good way along the Entiat River, then pine forest and more rustic mountain scenery take over. At the 6,600-foot elevation there is a viewpoint of great mountains with snow-topped Glacier Peak looming highest. The descent then begins to Lake Chelan, a road lined with wild flowers such as tansy, fireweed, Indian paintbrush, lupine, stonecrop, and yarrow.

Chelan County
apple orchard

109

Old Witte Homestead
near Winthrop,
Okanogan County

The road to Twisp
and Winthrop

I follow the Methow
River for some miles,
paralleling highways 153
and 20. Between Twisp
and Winthrop I sketch
the old Witte Homestead,
the Methow placidly flowing
past its back door. A broad
field of green alfalfa is in
the foreground and the
mountains of the Okanogan
National Forest grace the skyline.

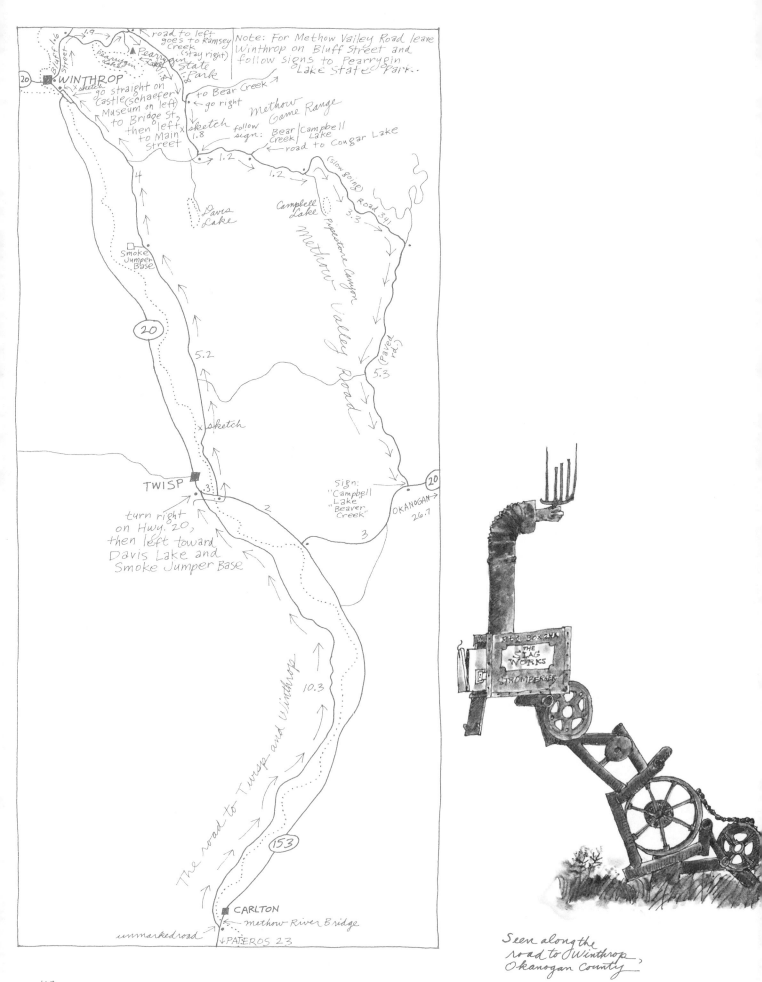

Note: For Methow Valley Road leave Winthrop on Bluff Street and follow signs to Pearrygin Lake State Park.

Bluff 1.6

1.9

road to left goes to Ramsey Creek (stay right)

Bluff Street

Pearrygin Lake State Park

20

WINTHROP

X sketch

go straight on Castle (Schaefer Museum on left) to Bridge St., then left to Main Street

to Bear Creek
go right

Methow Game Range

X sketch
1.8

follow sign:
Bear Creek | Campbell Lake
← road to Cougar Lake

4

1.2

1.2

Davis Lake

Campbell Lake

(slow going)

Road 34

3.3

Pipestone Canyon

Methow Valley Road

Smoke Jumper Base

20

5.2

(Paved rd.)
5.3

X sketch

TWISP

.3

Sign:
"Campbell Lake"
"Beaver Creek"

20

OKANOGAN →
26.7

turn right on Hwy. 20, then left toward Davis Lake and Smoke Jumper Base

2

3

The road to Twisp and Winthrop

10.3

153

CARLTON

← Methow River Bridge

unmarked road

↓ PATEROS 23

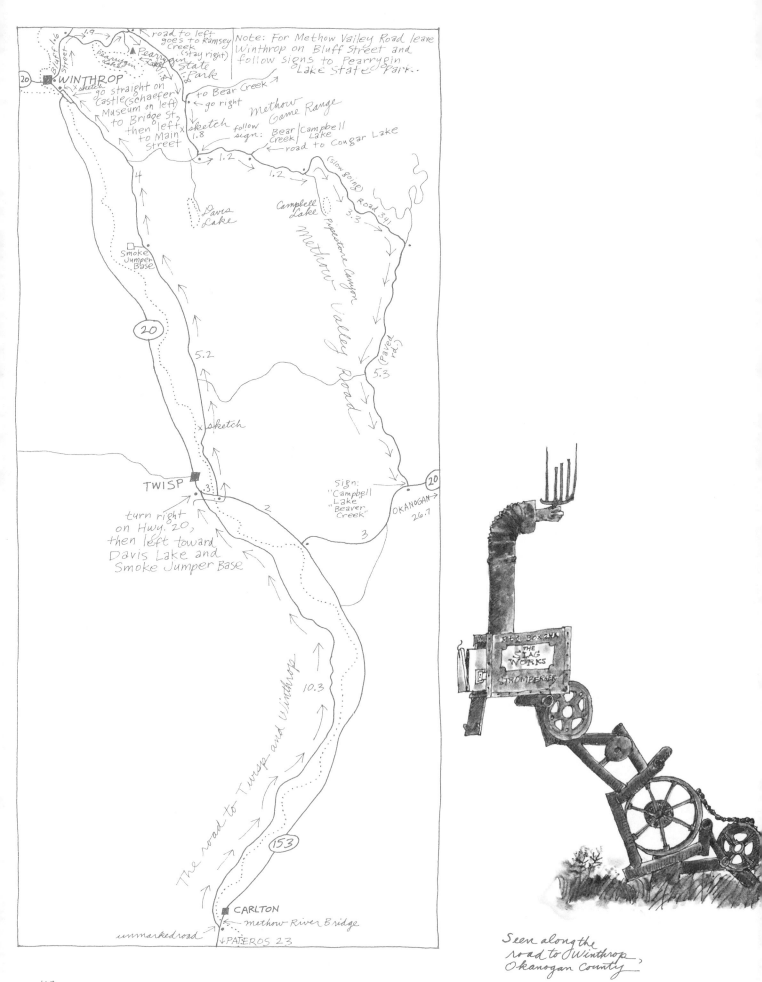

THE SLAG WORKS
R-1 BOX 2XX
STROMBERGS

Seen along the road to Winthrop, Okanogan County

At the Simon Schaefer Museum on Castle Avenue in Winthrop I draw the facade of an old log house complete with loafing homesteader. The museum is an entertaining stop with its collection of old buildings, antique farm equipment, and other historical items. And inside the museum I find a rare cookbook for sale, which includes a recipe for deep fried pigs' ears.

Buttercups,
Okanogan County

Old homesteader's cabin, Winthrop, Okanogan County

Back road
from
Winthrop

Goat Creek Road

sketch

20

Methow River   8.5

8.9

Chewack River

WINTHROP   cross bridge, follow sign to Sun Mt. and Fish Hatchery

FISH   .5
HATCHERY   .4
          .8   White
Twin Lakes   Ave.   20
Road

Back road from Winthrop

The road follows the Methow River through farming land and into primitive pine forest. Emerging from the thick forest I am back in farm country again. Sprinklers spray water all around, making green alfalfa crops still greener. Along the road I draw a chocolate-colored barn filled with golden-hued hay.

LOOMIS

Note: The trip was about 40 miles.

The road to Sinlahekin Valley

6.6

Sinlahekin Valley

Forde Lake

2.4

Sinlahekin Creek Road

2.4

Blue Lake

X sketch

3.6

1.3

Fish Lake

Sugarloaf

.8

follow sign to Conconully Lake and Loomis

4.3

Conconully Lake

WINTHROP

Okanogan National Forest

.3 CONCONULLY

State Park

3.1

Conconully Reservoir

1.1

OMAK 17

Rd 352B State Road Cabin campground

2.5

Rock Lake Road

7.9

Starvation Mountain 11

Rd 3621

Bucke Pass 5470'

Road 352

Lyda Camp

.8

Road 352

2.4

follow sign to Conconully

Loup Loup Campground

20

.5 TWISP 12

OKANOGAN 21.8

Loup Loup Summit

117

Methow Valley road
(map, page 112)
There are pleasing views of
mountains and valleys along this
road. I try to show this in my drawing
and to move the eye forward and back
again with overlapping ranges of hills,
farmland, forest, and mountain peaks.

View of Methow Valley
near Winthrop, Okanogan County

A good gravel road leads me through thick fir and pine forest to an old mining town once known as Salmon City. The more poetic name for this locale—Conconully—has survived. Translated from the Indian, it means "the beautiful land of the bunch grass flats."

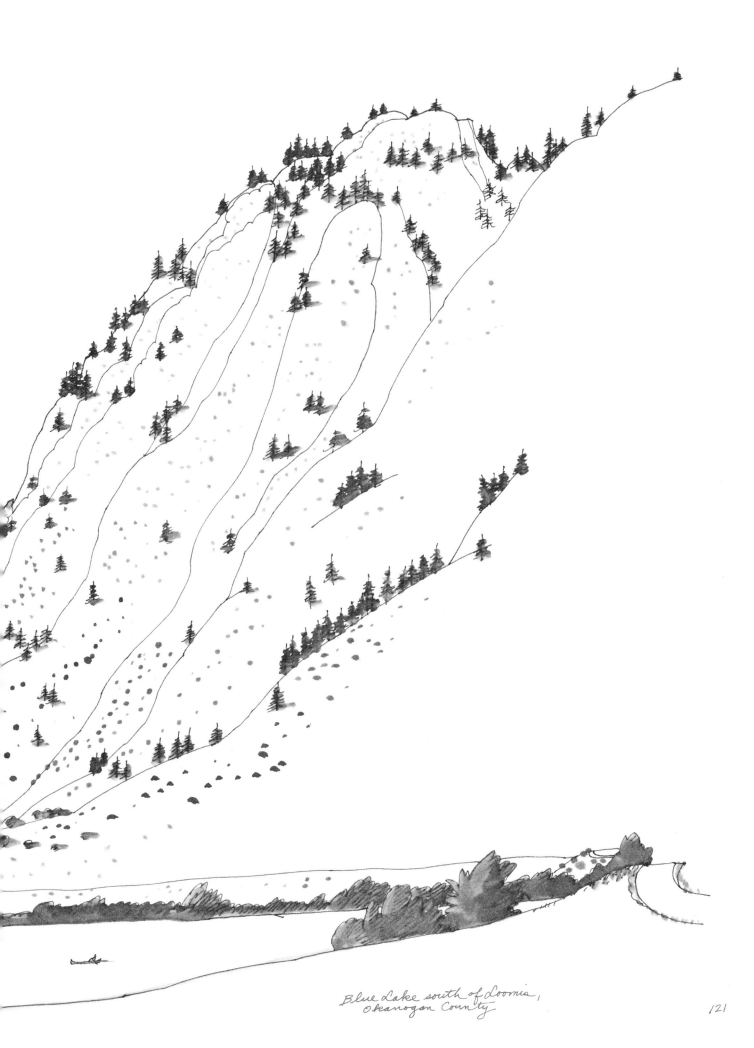

Blue Lake south of Loomis,
Okanogan County

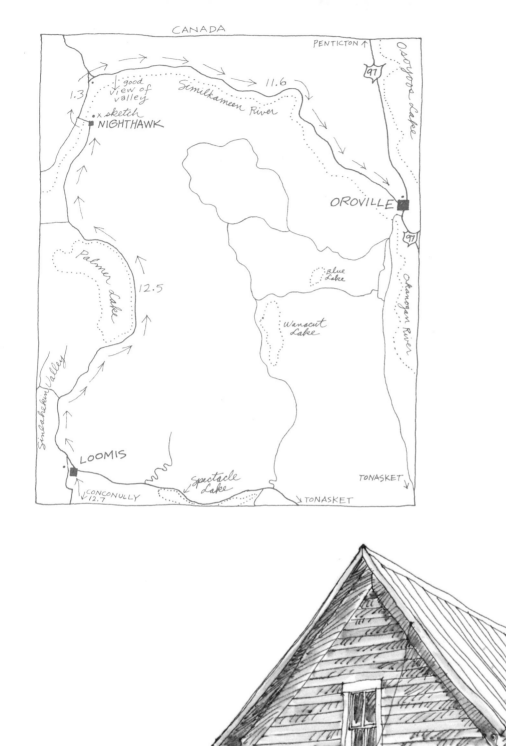

CANADA
PENTICTON ↑
97
Osoyoos Lake
good view of valley
1.3
x sketch
NIGHTHAWK
Similkameen River
11.6
OROVILLE
97
Palmer Lake
12.5
Okanogan River
Blue Lake
Wanacut Lake
Sinlahekin Valley
LOOMIS
Spectacle Lake
TONASKET
CONCONULLY 12.7
↓ TONASKET

*The Pink House, Nighthawk,
Okanogan County*

122

Loomis to Nighthawk and Oroville

Rock-faced mountains, dotted with pines and firs, abruptly rise in a colorful blend of blue, gray, purple, and ocher from Sinlahekin Valley north of Loomis. Apple orchards grow at one end of Palmer Lake, while green grass carpets the southern end of the valley.

At the almost deserted mining town of Nighthawk I sketch the Pink House. It had once been a lively hostelry and perhaps even a place of questionable repute, I was told by local folks. The old store and post office and the former hotel are still there and occupied. Discoveries of precious metal in the early 1890s made both Loomis and Nighthawk booming mining towns. The boom ended in a few years, but the scenic beauty of the valley remains.

The road to Oroville follows the Similkameen River, where gold was panned in 1857.

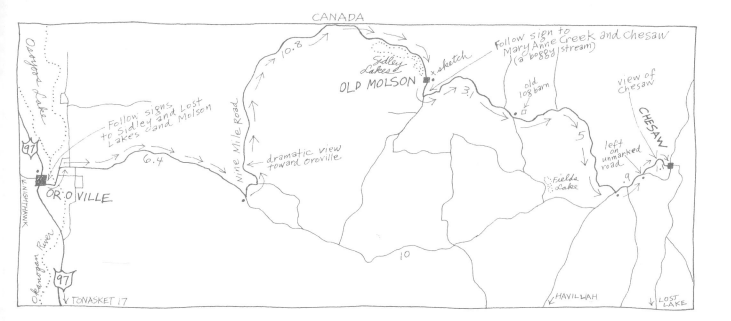

Road to Old Molson and Chesaw

The road parallels the Canadian border for almost a mile and later passes Sidley Lakes before entering Old Molson. Originally the town had a doctor, veterinarian, attorney, and a milliner; a drugstore, meat market, creamery, restaurant, furniture store, grocery store, harness shop, newspaper, and garage. When Kohrdt's Garage closed its doors for the last time in 1941, that was the end of Old Molson—except, of course, for the collection of early buildings, equipment, and memorabilia that remains there today.

Chesaw, too, has some of the same flavor. This town, once center of a mining district of over five hundred, claims it is named in honor of a Chinese miner named Joe Chee Saw.

OKANOGAN COUNTY HISTORICAL SOCIETY

OLD MOLSON

WELCOME FOLKS TO OLD MOLSON FOUNDED IN 1900. SHE WAS A LIVELY MINING CAMP UNTIL A FARMER CLAIMED THE WHOLE TOWN WAS PART OF HIS HOMESTEAD. WHILE THE DISPUTE RAGED, DISGUSTED CITIZENS FOUNDED NEW MOLSON HALF-A-MILE NORTH. PEOPLE, BUSINESSES, THE POST OFFICE - EVERYTHING MOVED TO NEW MOLSON. ITS RAILROAD STATION ELEV 3706 WAS THE HIGHEST IN THE STATE. THE ORIGINAL MOLSON FADED AWAY, BUT ITS MEMORIES LINGER IN THESE WEATHER-WORN BUILDINGS.

NO DOUBLE PARKING 3 HOUR PARKING LIMIT

DEPENDABLE CHAMPION SPARK PLUG SERVICE

THE STANDARD ZEROLENE FOR MOTOR CARS

AVOID PENALTY REPORT TO CUSTOMS VEHICLES ENTERING

Old Molson, Okanogan County

124

YE OLDE MOLSON
- 1900 -

MOLSON POST OFFICE

MOLSON STATE BANK

NO SMOKIN COPENHAGEN

125

Okanogan River road

Countless apple trees, branches laden with red and yellow fruit, a forest of wooden poles supporting them, adorn the green banks of the Okanogan River. There are also grassy meadows, river views, farms, and sparsely wooded bluffs along the way to Tonasket.

Okanogan River Valley,
Okanogan County

OROVILLE note:
.2 miles south
of Central Ave.
and Main St. turn
right on 12th
Ave (Wanacut
Lake Road)

.2

97

2.8

Wanacut
Lake

apple orchards

Okanogan River

7.6

←LOOMIS

ELLISFORD

1.1

River
Loop Road

1.1

4

sketch✗

Okanogan River

HAVILLAH →

Weller Road

TONASKET

20

WAUCONDA
23.7

97

5.3

County
Road
9437

OMAK 20

CHEWILIKAN
VALLEY

The road through Chewiliken Valley

Driving through rocky, sparse pine, and sagebrush country, I delight in the spectacular view of the Okanogan River winding its way through McLaughlin Canyon. On July 29, 1858, 149 miners led by James McLaughlin were ambushed by Indians in the canyon. One miner, Francis Wolff by name, could not control his horse. It galloped off without him in the direction of the ambushing Indians. He had packed $2,000 in gold dust on the creature and was determined not to lose it, so with great danger to himself, he managed to get the horse back in time (from the records of the Museum of Okanogan Historical Society). I sketch this grand view of quiet Chewiliken Valley. It has its own special beauty, with gray green sagebrush dotting the hills, golden grain crops in the valley, and distant dark green forest.

Chewiliken Valley,
Okanogan County

Lupine,
Okanogan County

The road
through
Chewilikan
Valley

TONASKET

20

WAUCONDA →
23.7

4

Take unmarked
road off 97 N. of river crossing

(turn left in
.3 miles to
McLaughlin Canyon
and Chewilikan
Valley)

Road 9437

1.3

good
view of
McLaughlin
Canyon

3.8 McLaughlin Canyon
Road
+ sketch

Hardy Road

3.6

97

20

1.3

"Riverside"
sign

Chewilikan
Valley

Okanogan
National Forest

Okanogan River

4.3

Chewilikan Valley Road

5.1

View of
Okanogan River

road
unmarked

Crawfish
Lake

Keystone Road

1.8

RIVERSIDE

Trink Creek Road

Okanogan River

97

20

9.5

OMAK

215

.6

.4

97

155

130

Balanced Rock,
Kartar Valley,
Okanogan County

Omak Lake Road

Attesting to Okanogan
County's great geological
variety, here at Omak Lake massive
rock formations jut majestically upward
from the blue green water. Along Kartar
Valley Road I sketch Balanced Rock
to the buzzing of bees and grasshoppers.
At Goose Lake there are plenty of
ducks among the bulrushes, and on
the road cows plump themselves
down and have to be nudged
up and along.

Omak Lake,
Okanogan County

The road to Nespelem and Republic

There is a dramatic view of the
Columbia River along this back road to
Nespelem. Once in town I visit the grave
of Chief Joseph, the famous war leader
of the Nez Percé Indians in the 1870s.
He led his people fifteen hundred miles
through Montana wilderness toward
Canada, but was captured at the border
by the United States Army. Finally sent
to Colville Reservation, he ended his
days in 1904 at Nespelem. Lettered
on his gravestone is his Indian
name, HIN-MAH-TOO-YAH-LAT-KEHT,
"Thunder rolling in the mountains."

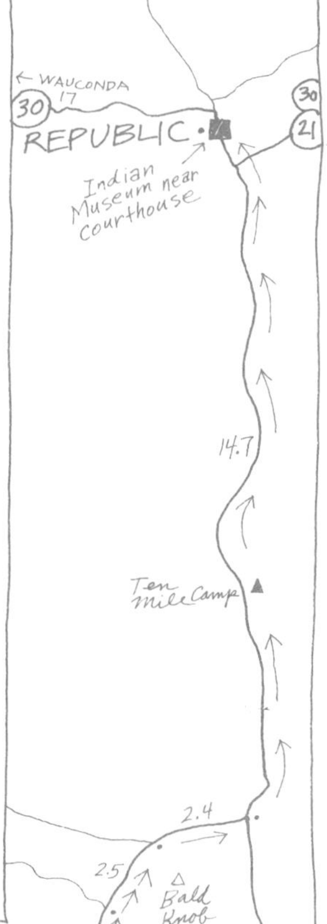

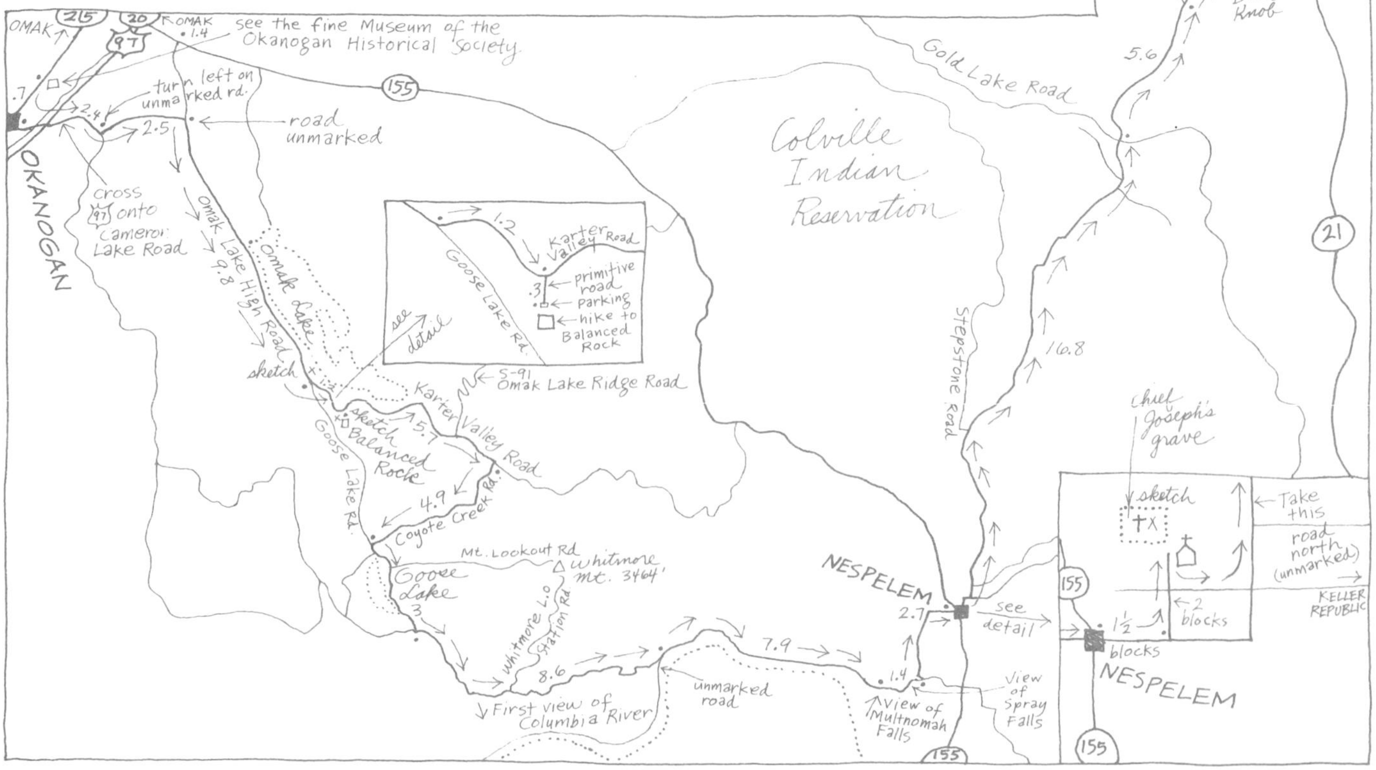

Map labels (top right):
← WAUCONDA
30 17
REPUBLIC
30
21
Indian Museum near courthouse
14.7
Ten mile Camp
2.4
2.5
Bald Knob
5.6
Gold Lake Road
21

Map labels (lower):
OMAK
215   20   OMAK 1.4   see the fine Museum of the
97   Okanogan Historical Society.
.7
2.4
2.5   road unmarked
turn left on unmarked rd.
155
cross 97 onto Cameron Lake Road
OKANOGAN
Omak Lake High Road 9.8
Omak Lake
sketch
Colville Indian Reservation
Karter Valley Road
1.2
Karter Valley Road
Primitive road
.3   Parking
hike to Balanced Rock
see detail
S-91 Omak Lake Ridge Road
sketch Balanced Rock
4.5
Goose Lake Rd.
4.9
Coyote Creek Rd.
Mt. Lookout Rd. Whitmore Mt. 3464'
Goose Lake .3
Whitmore L.O.
Station Rd.
8.6
7.9
First view of Columbia River
unmarked road
1.4
View of Multnomah Falls
View of Spray Falls
Stepstone road
16.8
Chief Joseph's grave
NESPELEM
2.7
see detail
155
sketch
†X
Take this road north (unmarked)
KELLER REPUBLIC
1½ blocks
2 blocks
NESPELEM
155

Headstone
at Nespelem,
Okanogan County

135

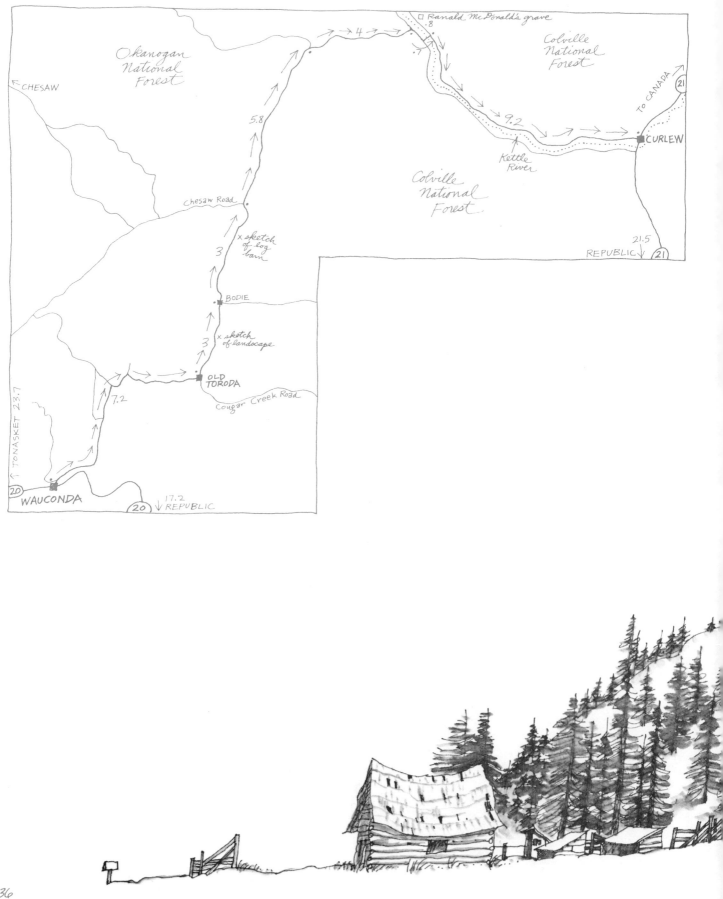

Okanogan
National
Forest

← CHESAW

5.8

Chesaw Road

x sketch
of log
barn

3

■ BODIE

x sketch
of landscape

3

■ OLD
TORODA

Cougar Creek Road

7.2

↑ TONASKET 23.7

(20)
WAUCONDA

(20) ↓ 17.2
↓ REPUBLIC

→ 4

□ Ranald McDonald's grave
.8

.7

Colville
National
Forest

TO CANADA → (21)

9.2

CURLEW

Kettle
River

Colville
National
Forest

21.5

REPUBLIC ↓ (21)

The road past Old Toroda

There are log homesteads at Old Toroda and a ghost town at Bodie. I sketch a swayback log house along the road, then discover a big log barn to draw at Single Shot Ranch a few miles past Bodie. Log barns and farmhouses give a quaint early American look to this narrow agricultural valley. Later, in Ferry County, during a very pretty drive along the Kettle River, I witness fly-fishermen trying their luck in the free-flowing stream. This brings me, finally, to the hamlet of Curlew.

Farm near Old Toroda,
Okanogan County

Log barn north of Bodie, Okanogan County

Back roads to and from Northport

From Orient, a back road goes past Little Pierre and Pierre Lakes. A fisherman at Pierre tells me he has fished cutthroat trout there since the 1930s. As he speaks, a great blue heron flies by chased by a hawk. Releasing plaintive cries all the while, the heron makes great maneuvers to escape the hawk. The road continues through thick forest, emerging eventually at Northport.

From Northport the scenery changes to views of the Columbia River and inland farms and woods. At Snag Cove I sketch the vast Franklin D. Roosevelt Lake portion of the Columbia River. Stalks of woolly mullein decorate the foreground of the picture.

Snag Cove,
Franklin D. Roosevelt Lake,
(Columbia River), Stevens County

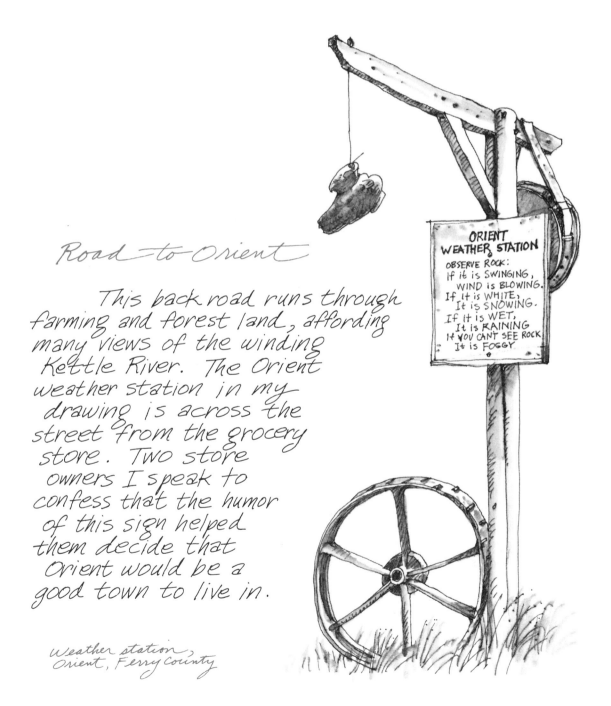

Road to Orient

This back road runs through farming and forest land, affording many views of the winding Kettle River. The Orient weather station in my drawing is across the street from the grocery store. Two store owners I speak to confess that the humor of this sign helped them decide that Orient would be a good town to live in.

Weather station, Orient, Ferry County

ORIENT
WEATHER STATION

OBSERVE ROCK:
If it is SWINGING,
  WIND is BLOWING.
If it is WHITE,
  It is SNOWING.
If it is WET,
  It is RAINING
If YOU CAN'T SEE ROCK
  It is FOGGY

The road past Deep Lake

Attractive meadows, old homesteads, and forest scenery are found on this trip north of Colville. Deep Lake, bathed in early morning mist, conveys a mood of serenity, calm, and mystery. Several miles farther north of Deep Lake, I sketch the 1804 Johnson homestead with its laundry spread along the fence. People settled in this valley along Deep Creek at that time to work in the local lead mines.

The old Johnson homestead,
Leadpoint, Stevens County

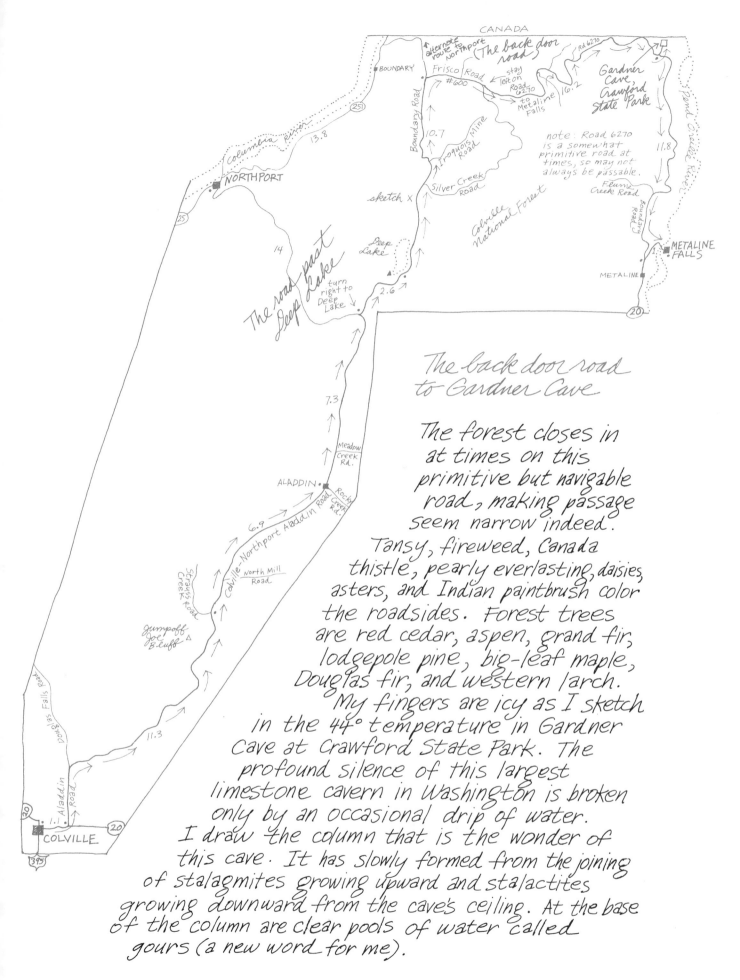

CANADA

alternate route to Northport

(The back door road)

Rd 6270

BOUNDARY

Frisco Road #600

stay left on Road 6270 to Metaline Falls

16.2

Gardner Cave, Crawford State Park

Boundary Road

Columbia River 13.8

10.7

Iroquois Mine Road

note: Road 6270 is a somewhat primitive road at times, so may not always be passable.

11.8

NORTHPORT

25

Silver Creek Road

sketch X

Colville National Forest

Flume Creek Road

Pend Oreille River

Boundary Road

METALINE FALLS

14

The road past Deep Lake

Deep Lake

METALINE

turn right to Deep Lake

2.6

20

7.3

Meadow Creek Rd.

ALADDIN

Rocky Creek Rd.

6.9

Colville-Northport Aladdin Road

North Mill Road

Strawls Road

Jumpoff Joe B. Cliff

Douglas Falls Road

11.3

20

1.1

Aladdin Road

COLVILLE

395

The back door road to Gardner Cave

The forest closes in at times on this primitive but navigable road, making passage seem narrow indeed.
  Tansy, fireweed, Canada thistle, pearly everlasting, daisies, asters, and Indian paintbrush color the roadsides. Forest trees are red cedar, aspen, grand fir, lodgepole pine, big-leaf maple, Douglas fir, and western larch.
  My fingers are icy as I sketch in the 44° temperature in Gardner Cave at Crawford State Park. The profound silence of this largest limestone cavern in Washington is broken only by an occasional drip of water.
  I draw the column that is the wonder of this cave. It has slowly formed from the joining of stalagmites growing upward and stalactites growing downward from the cave's ceiling. At the base of the column are clear pools of water called gours (a new word for me).

146

Gardner Cave
near Metaline Falls,
Pend Oreille
County

147

Road to Manresa Grotto

From Metaline Falls, the road runs through forests, hugging the edge of the deep blue water of Sullivan Lake and south of Ione following the picturesque Pend Oreille River.

At Manresa Grotto, on the Kalispel Indian Reservation, I sketch the cool gray interior of this natural cathedral formed by solid rock. Established by Catholic priest Father Dement, it is a place that inspires worship and meditation, and was revered by the Kalispel Indian tribe (despite hard rock seats).

Manresa Grotto,
Pend Oreille County

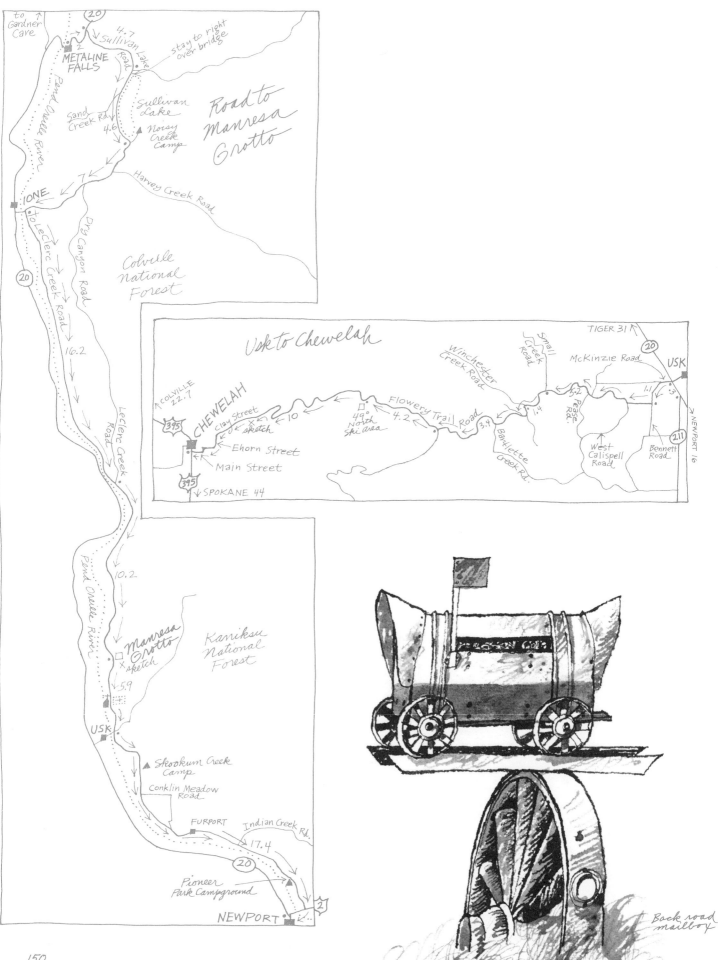

to
Gardner
Cave

20

4.7
Sullivan Lake Road

stay to right
over bridge

METALINE
FALLS

Sand Creek Rd.
4.6

Sullivan
Lake

Noisy
Creek
Camp

Road to
Manresa
Grotto

Pend Oreille River

.7

Harvey Creek Road

IONE

to LeClerc Creek Road

Dry Canyon Road

Colville
National
Forest

20

16.2

LeClerc Creek Road

Usk to Chewelah

TIGER 31

Small Creek Road

20

Winchester Creek Road

McKinzie Road

USK

COLVILLE 22.7

CHEWELAH

Flowery Trail Road

5.2

1.1

.3

395

Clay Street
sketch

10

49°
North
Ski area

4.2

1.4

Pease Rd.

NEWPORT 16

Ehorn Street

3.4

211

Main Street

Bartlette Creek Rd.

West
Calispell
Road

Bennett
Road

395

SPOKANE 44

10.2

Pend Oreille River

Manresa
Grotto
sketch

Kaniksu
National
Forest

5.9

USK

Skookum Creek
Camp

Conklin Meadow
Road

FURPORT

Indian Creek Rd.

17.4

20

Pioneer
Park Campground

2

NEWPORT

150

Back road
mailbox

Back road
musician

Usk to Chewelah (map page 150)

The road from Usk passes through farm and forest landscape and up to the 49° North ski area, then back down again to the pleasant town of Chewelah. I draw the barn at Davidson's farm on the way. Coyotes yowl from the forest and a herd of sheep come munching into the picture. I didn't draw them because they weren't supposed to be there. Mrs. Davidson has to get in her car and drive to the neighbors' house to tell them that their sheep are loose. Some boys chase the sheep back, but an hour later I observe them again munching their way onto the Davidson property.

Davidson's Farm
near Chewelah,
Stevens County

153

154

Back road through Colville Valley

There is great agricultural beauty to behold along this interesting back road— the patterns and textures of the crops, the sweeping lines of agricultural divisions. My reward for sitting quietly as I draw this farm scene is a magnificent, multicolored dragonfly that perches on my drawing board. I am extremely pleased to have inspired confidence in such an elegant member of the insect world.

Ranch in Colville Valley,
Stevens County

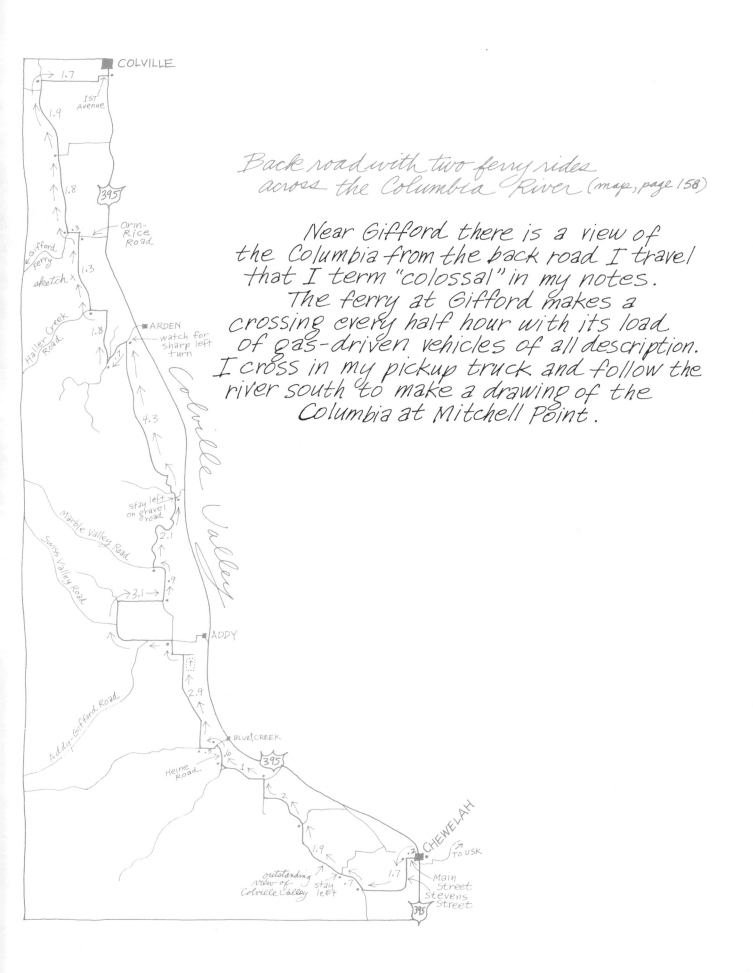

Back road with two ferry rides across the Columbia River (map, page 158)

Near Gifford there is a view of the Columbia from the back road I travel that I term "colossal" in my notes.

The ferry at Gifford makes a crossing every half hour with its load of gas-driven vehicles of all description. I cross in my pickup truck and follow the river south to make a drawing of the Columbia at Mitchell Point.

COLVILLE

1.7

1ST Avenue

1.9

1.8

395

Orin-Rice Road

.3

Gifford ferry

sketch X

1.3

Haller Creek Road

1.8

ARDEN
watch for sharp left turn

.1

4.3

Colville Valley

stay left on gravel road

2.1

Marble Valley Road

Suss Valley Road

.9

→3.1→

ADDY

2.9

Addy-Gifford Road

BLUE CREEK

.6

Heine Road

←1

395

2

1.9

CHEWELAH

.2

TO USK

.7

outstanding view of Colville Valley

stay left

1.7

Main Street
Stevens Street

395

The Columbia River,
Mitchell Point,
Colville Indian Reservation,
Ferry County

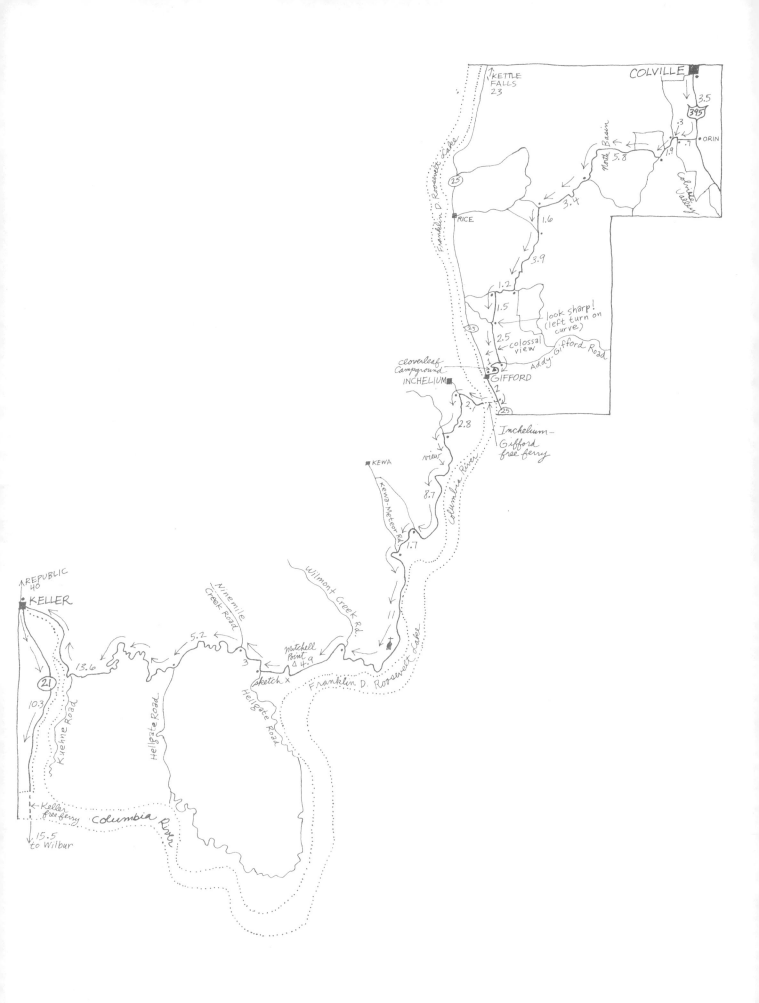

COLVILLE

↑KETTLE
FALLS
23

3.5

395

.3

.1 • ORIN

1.9

North Basin

5.8

Colville Valley

3.4

■ RICE

1.6

Franklin D. Roosevelt Lake

25

3.9

1.2

1.5

look sharp!
(left turn on
curve)

25

2.5

colossal
view

Addy-Gifford Road

cloverleaf
Campground
INCHELIUM■

GIFFORD

2

25

2.1

Inchelium-
Gifford
free ferry

2.8

■ KEWA

view

Columbia River

8.7

Kewa-Meteor Rd.

1.7

Wilmont Creek Rd.

11

↑REPUBLIC
40

KELLER■

Ninemile
Creek Road

5.2

Mitchell
Point
△ 4.9

Franklin D. Roosevelt Lake

13.6

3

sketch ×

21

Kuehne Road

Hellgate Road

Hellgate Road

10.3

←Keller
free ferry

Columbia River

↓15.5
to Wilbur

The Keller ferry ride at the end
of the back road trip through Colville
Indian country is delightful. I take
it four times in order to make the
drawing. During the eleven years
two operators worked the ferry,
bad weather halted its operation
on only one occasion. They
like their job but admit it
could be a bitterly cold crossing
in midwinter.

"Martha S," the ferry
across Columbia River,
Ferry and Lincoln Counties

The road to Hartline

From Grand Coulee the road winds through a rocky, sagebrush-covered draw. There is a large view of Grand Coulee dam, then a great rolling landscape plateau of wheatland all around. The horizon line is broken here and there by a lone barn, farm, and windmill and by an old silo like this one sketched near the grain elevator town of Hartline.

Back road mailbox

Old silo near Hartline, Grant County

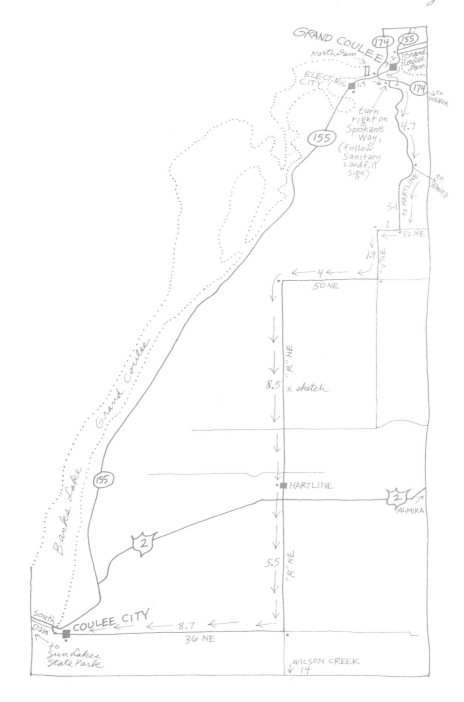

Back road loop from Coulee City

To irrigate the farmlands of Washington,
Summer Falls charges over this parapet of stone
with thundering force. A hydroelectric generating
facility will be placed here, a nearby notice reads.
It may mean that the Falls will be eliminated,
but in the meantime it is exciting to witness all
that water seething, roiling, roaring, booming
into Billy Clapp Lake.

The cliffs and sagebrush of Dry Coulee
Road bring to mind scenery from movies of the
Old West.

At Wilson Creek, where Zack Finney
started the first school in 1892, and where an
immigrant train arrived from Minnesota in 1901, there
is a lovely shaded park just perfect for a picnic.

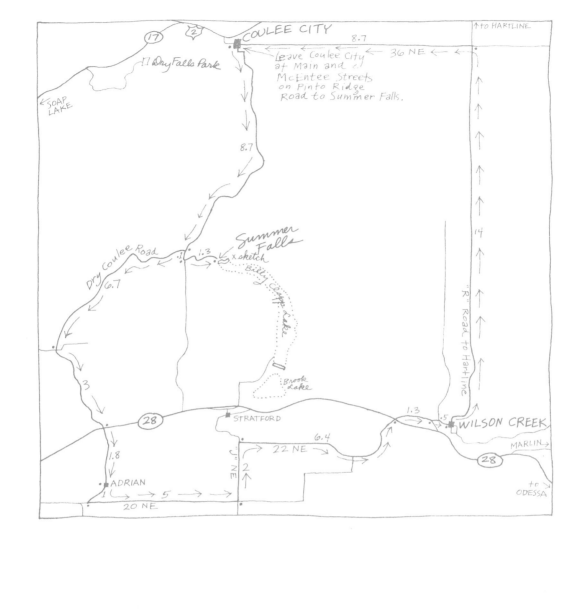

17　⌂2　COULEE CITY　8.7

← Leave Coulee City ← 36 NE ←
at Main and ⌂
McEntee Streets
on Pinto Ridge
Road to Summer Falls.

↑ to HARTLINE

‖ Dry Falls Park

SOAP LAKE

8.7

Summer Falls

Dry Coulee Road　.1　1.3　X sketch

6.7

Billy Clapp Lake

14

"R" Road to Hartline

Brook Lake

3

28　■ STRATFORD　1.3　.5　■ WILSON CREEK

6.4

22 NE

MARLIN →

1.8　　J NE　2　　28

ADRIAN

to ODESSA

1　5 →
20 NE

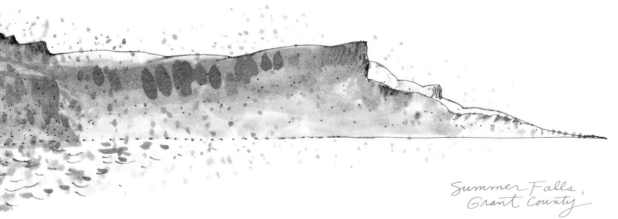

Summer Falls,
Grant County

Roadside
sunflower,
Stevens County

164

Road along the Spokane River

The Spokane Indian reservation road cuts through pine forest and meadow. Now I drive along the Spokane River itself and enjoy a landscape of green crops, river views, occasional farms, and roadside sunflowers in abundance.

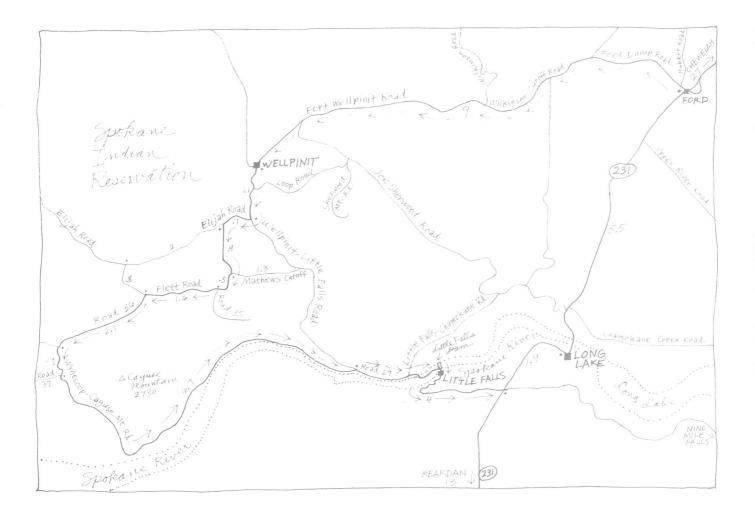

Dalmatian
Toadflax,
Spokane
County

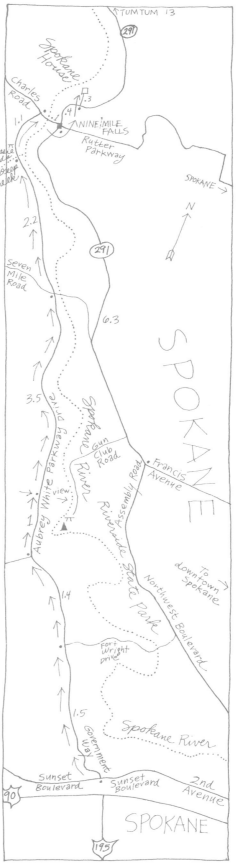

There is a splendid view of Spokane from the ridge along this forest and river road. I explore Deep Creek Canyon and find a variety of wild flowers. I make studies of two common tansy, with its bright yellow flower heads resembling golden buttons, and a yellow flower with the incredible name of Dalmatian toadflax. Spokane House Interpretive Center can be visited at the end of the trip. It is the site of an 1810 trading post and the first permanent white settlement in Washington.

Tansy, Spokane County

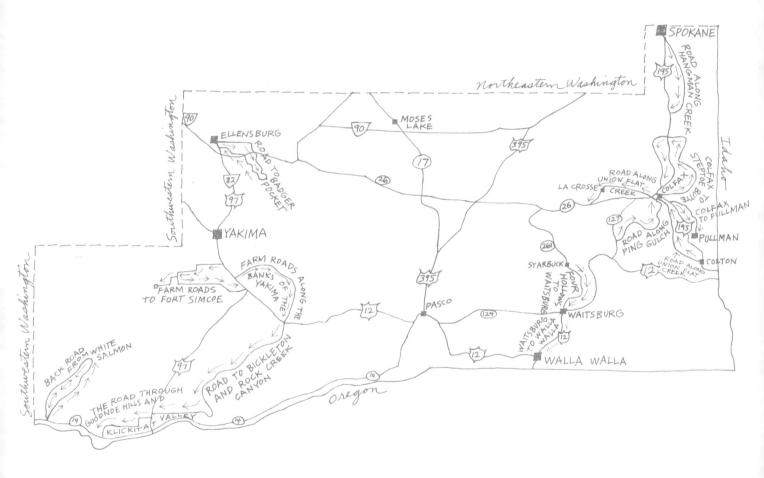

SPOKANE

ROAD ALONG HANGMAN CREEK

Northeastern Washington

195

Idaho

Southwestern Washington

90

ELLENSBURG

MOSES LAKE

90

17

395

82

97

ROAD TO BADGER POCKET

26

COLFAX STEPTOE BUTTE

ROAD ALONG UNION FLAT CREEK

LA CROSSE

COLFAX

26

COLFAX TO PULLMAN

YAKIMA

121

ROAD ALONG PING GULCH

195

PULLMAN

261

FARM ROADS ALONG THE BANKS OF THE YAKIMA

STARBUCK

FOUR HOLLOWS TO WAITSBURG

ROAD ALONG UNION FLAT

COLTON

12

FARM ROADS TO FORT SIMCOE

395

PASCO

124

WAITSBURG

WAITSBURG TO WALLA WALLA

BACK ROAD FROM WHITE SALMON

12

12

WAITSBURG TO WALLA WALLA

97

ROAD TO BICKLETON AND ROCK CREEK CANYON

12

WALLA WALLA

THE ROAD THROUGH GOODNOE HILLS AND KLICKITAT VALLEY

14

14

Oregon

14

Southwestern Washington

Southeastern Washington

I recall the fruit trees, grapevines, and the tall green of hops in Yakima Valley; the peas, asparagus, and sweet onion fields of Walla Walla; the dairy and grain country around Ellensburg, and the rolling wheatlands south of Spokane. And in late summer there is the drama of the harvest. By traveling the back roads, I witness the great agricultural achievement of the land.

Giant Blazing Star
(bright yellow flowers),
Klickitat County

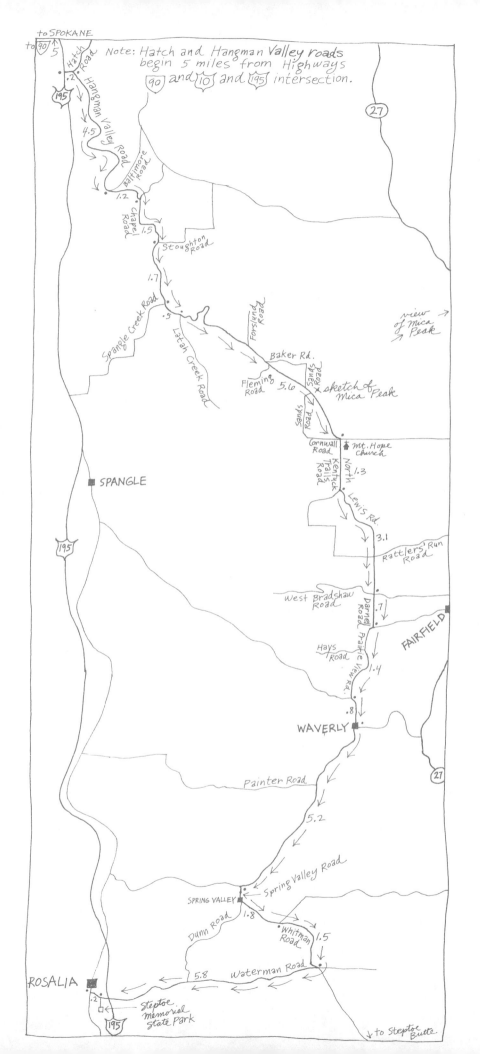

Note: Hatch and Hangman Valley roads begin 5 miles from Highways 90 and 10 and 195 intersection.

to SPOKANE
to 90 | 5
Hatch Road
.2
195
Hangman Valley Road
4.5
Baltimore Road
1.2
Chapel Road
1.5
Stoughton Road
1.7
Spangle Creek Road
.5
Latah Creek Road
Forslund Road
Baker Rd.
Fleming Road
5.6
Sands Road
Sands Road
Cornwall Road
Mt. Hope Church
Kentuck Trails Road
North
1.3
Lewis Rd.
3.1
Rattlers' Run Road
West Bradshaw Road
.7
Darnell Road
Prairie View Rd.
FAIRFIELD
Hays Road
1.4
27
WAVERLY
.8

view of Mica Peak →

sketch of Mica Peak

SPANGLE

195

Painter Road
5.2
Spring Valley Road
SPRING VALLEY
1.8
Dunn Road
Whitman Road
1.5
Waterman Road
5.8
ROSALIA
.2
Steptoe Memorial State Park
195
↓ to Steptoe Butte

The road along Hangman Creek

    Hangman Creek Road soon brings me to the rolling grain and grass seed fields south of Spokane. From one vista point I sketch Mica Peak and the extensive agricultural land surrounding it. Bluegrass fields are being burned in the distance, the smoke threatening the visibility of the mountain. The sound of harvesting machinery fills the air from beyond the nearby hills.

Harvester,
Spokane County

Mica Peak,
Spokane County

Road along Ping Gulch

From the campground along the Snake River at Central Ferry I see tugs pushing loaded barges. They carry oil, grain, fish, and wood—a variety of products from Idaho. An incredibly long freight train creaks over a trestle suspended high above the Snake. An image of Buster Keaton racing and leaping from car to car comes to mind. I am occupied counting cars for quite a while, for it turns out there are a hundred of them!

In Ping Gulch there are cows, rolling wheatlands, creekside willows, roadside sunflowers, neat farmhouses, and dogs running alongside my vehicle.

Ping Gulch ranch,
Garfield County

At Lower Granite Lock and Dam on the Snake River
I visit the Fish Viewing Room and the fish ladder. There
are steelhead trout, channel catfish, carp, salmon, and
many other fish to see.

The hills roll gracefully on either side of the
road to Colfax. I feel that I am gaining more
knowledge of the land and its farming people
for taking this meandering series of back
country roads.

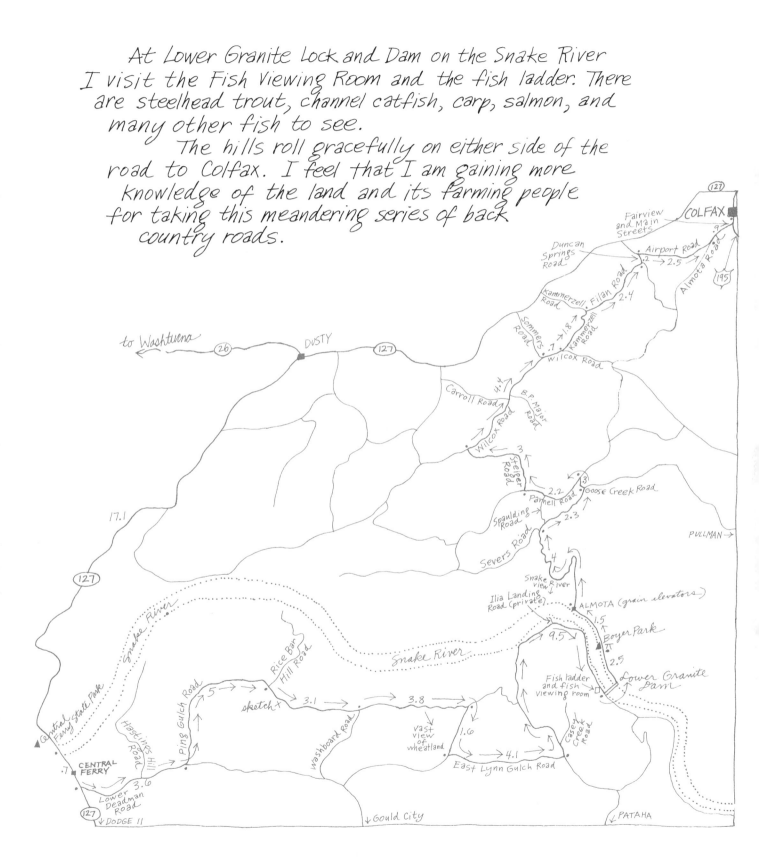

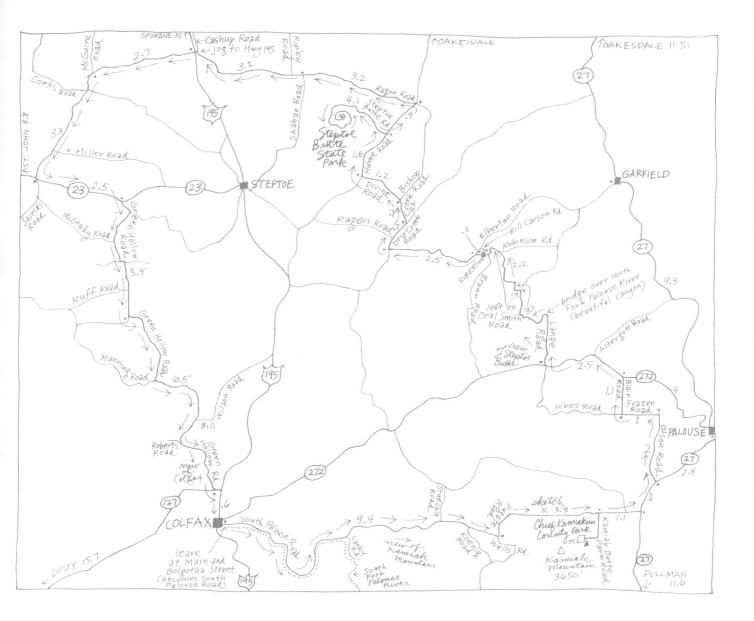

Colfax to Steptoe Butte

I follow the Palouse River past well-kept farmhouses, their gardens adorned with flowers. Near Kamiak Butte I make a drawing of the rolling farmland. Kamiak was a famous Yakima Indian chieftain, and the butte named after him is now a county park. I cross the Palouse River, here flowing through a deep canyon, and proceed to the picturesque community of Elberton. Later, as I appreciate the view from atop Steptoe Butte, I reflect on the geology of this region. I am looking down from an ancient mountain that ten million years ago was

Surrounded by lava flows. Kamiak Butte is another old mountain that lava had surrounded but not covered. The rich covering of dirt and topsoil, layered over the old lava flows, today support the Palouse area's large-scale dry farming of peas, lentils, and wheat.

Landscape near Colfax, Whitman County

177

Country road from Colfax to Pullman

In Colfax, on Perkins Avenue near Last Street, you can see the 1884 Victorian house of the first permanent resident of the town, James A. Perkins. (If you wish to see the interior, write to the Whitman County Historical Society, Box 447, Pullman.)

The farmland in this area was once covered with bunchgrass. Early settlers called it palouse, from the French word for short, thick grass.

In a quiet valley I sketch the McIntosh Angus Ranch red barn and house. The black angus pictured here is particularly clean, for it has just been washed by a member of the McIntosh family. Other back roads beckon me to the delightful university town of Pullman, at the junction of the three forks of the Palouse River.

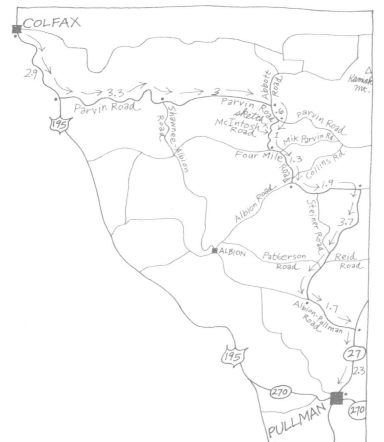

COLFAX
2.9
3.3
3
Parvin Road
Abbott Road
Kamiak Mt.
Parvin Road
sketch
McIntosh Road
195
Shawnee-Albion Road
.6
Mik Parvin Rd.
1
Four Mile Road
1.3
Collins Rd.
1.9
Albion Road
Steiner Road
3.7
ALBION
Patterson Road
Reid Road
1.7
Albion-Pullman Road
195
27
2.3
270
PULLMAN
270

McIntosh Angus Ranch,
Whitman County

Grain elevator,
Union Flat Creek Road,
Whitman County

Within the map inset:

Union Flat Creek sketch

Union Flat Creek Rd.

Jim Knott Road

Endicott SW Road

Union Flat Creek

15.6

Long John Morasch Rd.

Luft Road

Winona South Road

Gaske Road

6.4

LA CROSSE

26

26

WASHTUCNA 21

The road along Union Flat Creek

I proceed through valley landscape past handsome farms and big barns. Willow trees grow along the creek. Klemgard County Park is situated on an attractive site for picnicking.

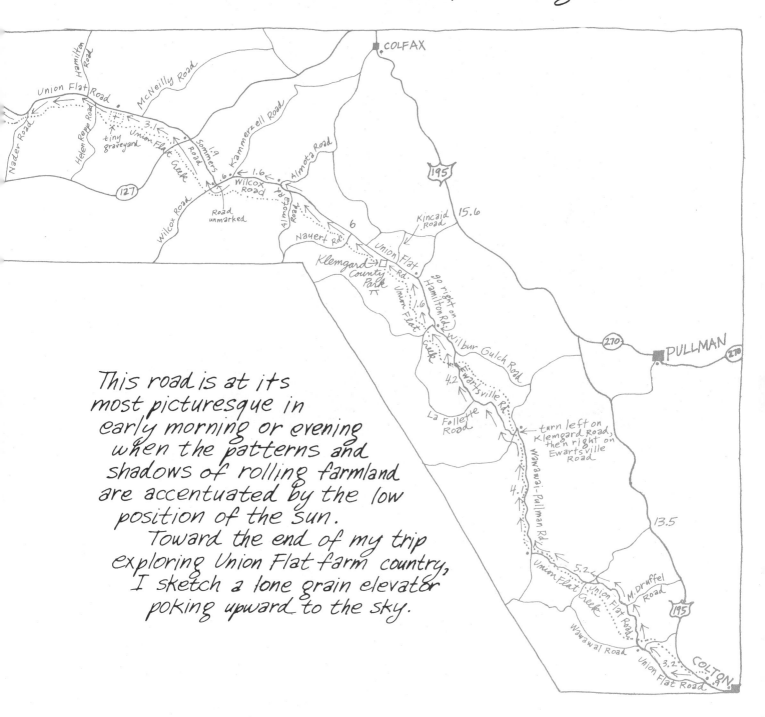

This road is at its most picturesque in early morning or evening when the patterns and shadows of rolling farmland are accentuated by the low position of the sun.

Toward the end of my trip exploring Union Flat farm country, I sketch a lone grain elevator poking upward to the sky.

1892 Drugstore,
Waitsburg
Walla Walla
County

Four Hollows to Waitsburg

    South of Washtucna, Adams County, are two
well-maintained state parks: Palouse Falls and Lyons Ferry.
Crossing the Snake River at Lyons Ferry, I travel
back roads with names like Smith Hollow, Whetstone Hollow,
Thorn Hollow, Sorghum Hollow, and even Whoopemup Hollow.

Near Waitsburg, on Highway 12, is Lewis and Clark Trail State Park, where in May 1806, Lewis and Clark's party ate parsnips and dog meat, having nothing else to choose from. In historic Waitsburg I sketch two facades in the well-preserved old town. At the local newspaper, the _Times,_ the editor informs me that the paper's 1888 building once had a decorative design at the top that has long since been removed. He suspects that the lawyer who used to have his office there had the peaked and turreted top taken off when the bricks and mortar began to show some wear. The lawyer, he conjectured, had been trying to avoid suit should a brick dislodge and fall on a passerby. However, the editor studied the prevailing wind direction, and it

THE TIMES

The Times, Waitsburg, Walla Walla County

was his conclusion that should any part have deteriorated enough to fall, it would have fallen in the direction of the roof, not the street. The missing top accounted for the building's rather blunt roof line.

J.W. Morgan's 1892 drugstore has today been put to another use, but the well-proportioned, early Waitsburg design is still almost intact. Testimony to Waitsburg's interest in preserving its heritage of history is the Bruce Memorial Museum, at 4th and Main streets, which should also be seen while you are in town.

Waitsburg to Walla Walla

This road takes me through the agricultural land north of Walla Walla, then east of the city to the "walk-in entrance" of Whitman Mission. It is a peaceful place of great beauty, but it is also the site of the massacre of the missionary Marcus Whitman family and other mission members by Cayuse Indians in 1847. The Cayuse had their reasons: one of them was that white settlers visiting the mission had transmitted a measles epidemic to the Indians that had wiped out half their tribe! When a cure could not be found by missionary-doctor Whitman, the Indians lost faith in the Whitman cause. There is more to the dramatic story; it awaits you at the Whitman Mission.

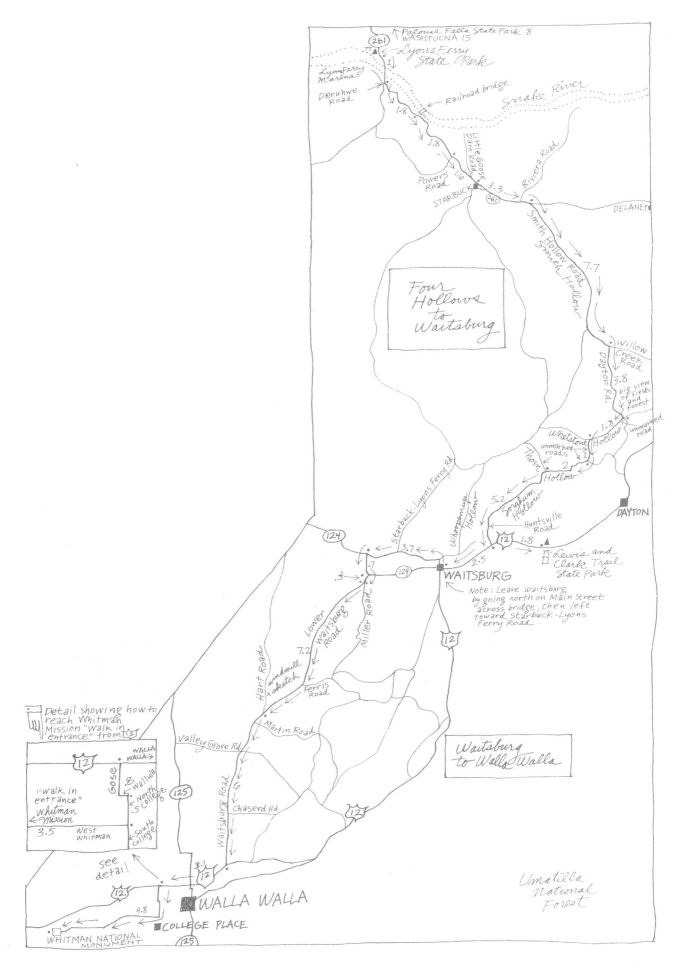

Palouse Falls State Park 8
WASHTUCNA 15
(261)
Lyons Ferry State Park
Lyons Ferry Marina
Deruhwe Road
1.
1.8
Railroad bridge
Snake River
2.8
Little Goose Dam Road
Powers Road 1.6
3.3
STARBUCK (261)
Riviera Road
DELANEY
Smith Hollow Road
Smith Hollow
7.7

Four Hollows to Waitsburg

Willow Creek Road
3.8 big view of fields and forest
Dayton Rd.
Whetstone Hollow 1.8
unmarked road
unmarked roads 1
Thorn Hollow 2
5.2 Sorghum Hollow
Whoopemup Hollow
Huntsville Road
DAYTON
(124)
Starbuck-Lyons Ferry Rd.
3.7
(12) 1.8
Lewis and Clark Trail State Park
.7
(124)
2.5
WAITSBURG
Note: Leave Waitsburg by going north on Main Street across bridge, then left toward Starbuck-Lyons Ferry Road.
.3
Lower Waitsburg Road
Miller Road
(12)
Hart Road
7.2
windmill sketch
Ferris Road
Martin Road

Waitsburg to Walla Walla

Detail showing how to reach Whitman Mission "walk in entrance" from 12
WALLA WALLA →
(12)
Gose
.8 Wallula
North College .5
"walk in entrance" Whitman Mission →
3.5 West Whitman
South College
(125)
Valley Grove Rd.
Chaserd Rd.
Waitsburg Road
.6
(12)
see detail
3.1
(12)
(12)
4.8
WALLA WALLA
COLLEGE PLACE
WHITMAN NATIONAL MONUMENT
(125)

Umatilla National Forest

185

The road to Badger Pocket.

Frail ninety-year-old Clareta Olmstead shows me the old cottonwood log cabin built by the Olmstead family in 1875. Its historic furnishings include an 1870 Scottish spinning wheel. It is now part of a state park and is open to visitors most of the year. There are many other turn-of-the-century buildings in addition to the log cabin. As I sketch, peacocks strut about the grounds occasionally giving off plaintive, loud, babylike cries.

Olmstead Cabin, 1875,
Kittitas County

ELLENSBURG

90

CLE ELUM
23

Mt. View Road   4   #6 Road   2.2   KITTITAS

.8

821 .3

Berry Rd.

Bull Rd.

1.1

Tjossem Road   Tjossem Road   1.3

1.6

82

97

Olmstead Cabin

Squaw Creek

.8

90

4th Ave and Main

Railroad Avenue

1.1

.4 Badger Pocket Road

1.3

Cleman Road

Carroll Road   1.4

Mundy Road

Vantage

VANTAGE
21

90

Moe Road

2.1

Ferguson Rd.

Sorenson Road

Emerson Road   1.3

Billeter Rd.

2.5

Oda Johnson Rd.

Hamilton Road

Badger

Badger

Prater Road

1.2

E. Larsen Road

1

1

Boch Road

Pocket Road

Pocket

A. Larsen Road

Bare Rd.

1

4th Parallel Road

#6 Road

Thrall Road

Denmark Road

Les Wilson Rd

4th Parallel Rd

X sketch

5.5

B. Clerf Road

.9

Ditchbank Road

1.1

Morrison Rd.

.5

Hayes Road

Manastash Ridge

821

Katen Rd.

W. Pet Rd.

Katen Rd.

Badger Pocket Road

Borland Road

Ross Rd.

.6

Bynum Rd.

Dead end

YAKIMA   YAKIMA 32

Badger Pocket landscape,
near Ellensburg, Kittitas County

188

Following this visit I explore Badger Pocket, where green farmland pushes up into the sagebrush-covered surrounding hills. This is rich dairyland, and green and golden hay crops and Hereford cattle are in plenitude.

Ellensburg, called Robber's Roost in 1870, contains many historic buildings. You should obtain a map showing them at the Chamber of Commerce.

Farm roads to Fort Simcoe

Past apple and peach orchards, pastureland, fields of mint, corn, and hay, these roads finally lead to Fort Simcoe. Located on the Yakima Indian Reservation, the fort was originally built to oversee the Indians and to protect Yakima Treaty areas from land-hungry settlers.

I liked Fort Simcoe for its spacious lawns and venerable oaks. The Yakimas called the location Mool Mool, a place of bubbling springs.

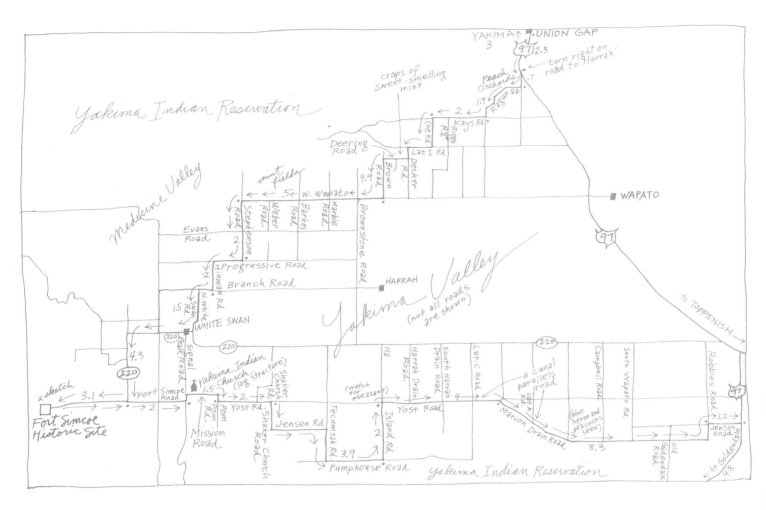

Yakima Indian Reservation

YAKIMA ↑ — UNION GAP
3 — [97] 2.3
"turn right on road to Harrah"
.7
crops of sweet-smelling mint
Peach Orchards
1.9 — Ragan Rd.
← 2 — Kays Rd.
Coe Rd. — Kripes Rd.
Deering Road
Lat 1 Rd.
Brown Rd. — Decker Rd.
4.9
mint fields
← 5 — W. Wapato
Stephenson Road — Weber Road — Barkes Road — Marble Road
Brown Stone Road
Medicine Valley
Evans Road
2
Hannah Rd. — Progressive Road
Branch Road
HARRAH
1.5 — Swan Rd. — N. White Rd.
WHITE SWAN
(220)
Yakima Valley
(not all roads are shown)

WAPATO

[97]

to TOPPENISH →

(220)

4.3
[220]
Peak Road — Signal
Yakima Indian Church (log structure)
1.5
2 — Shaker Church Rd.
Ha Rd. — Harrah Drain Road — South Harrah Drain Road — Lat-C Road
a canal parallels road
Campbell Road — South Wapato Rd.
Robbins Road

x sketch
← 3.1 — ↓ Fort Simcoe Road
→ • → 2 → • →
Pom Rd.
Yost Rd.
(watch for pheasant)
Yost Road
4
Lat. D Rd.
Marion Drain Road
(blue heron and peacocks seen)
8.3
Old Goldendale Road
1.2
Jenson Road
[97]

Fort Simcoe Historic Site

Mission Road
Shaker Church Road
Jensen Rd
Tecumseh Rd. — Island Rd.
3.9
2
Pumphouse Road
Yakima Indian Reservation
to Goldendale → 48

Fort Simcoe Historical Site,
Yakima County

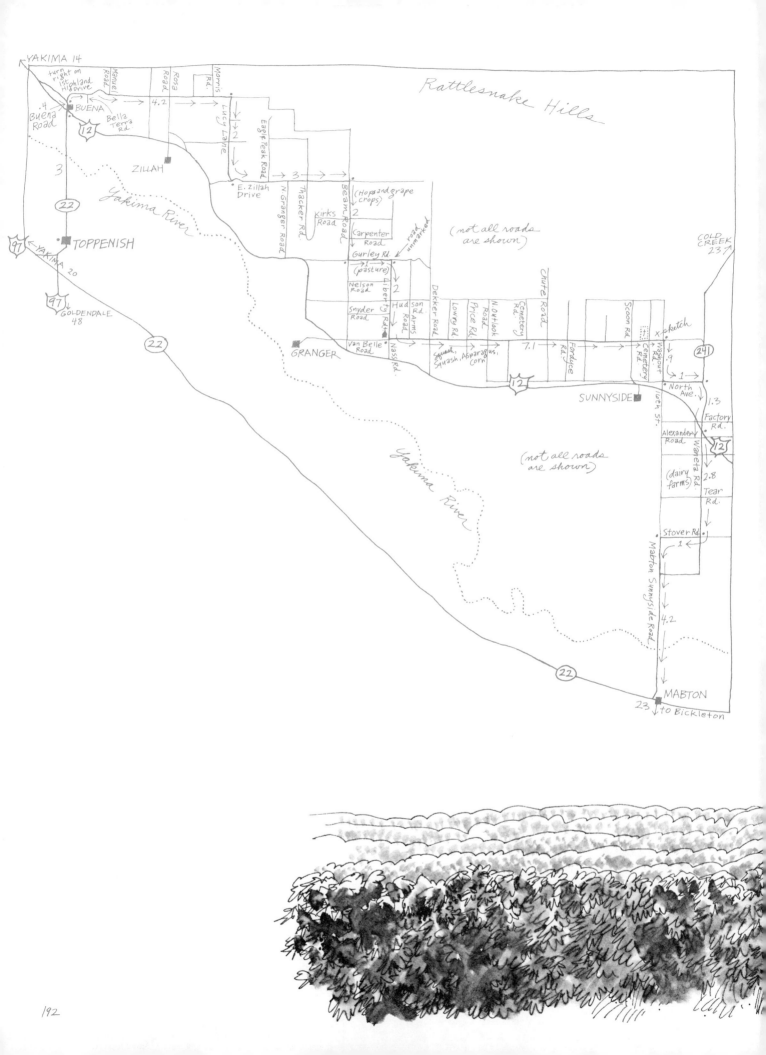

YAKIMA 14

turn right on 1st Highland Hi. Drive

Manuel Road

Rosa Road

Morris Rd.

.4
Buena Road · BUENA
Bella Terra Rd.

(12)

4.2 →

Lucy Lane

↓ 2 ↓

Eagle Peak Road

↓

Rattlesnake Hills

3

(22)

ZILLAH

E. Zillah Drive

N. Granger Road

Thacker Rd.

Kirks Road

Beam Road

3 →

(Hops and grape crops)

2

Carpenter Road

Gurley Rd.

road unmarked

(not all roads are shown)

COLD CREEK 23.7

(97)

Yakima River

TOPPENISH

Yakima 20

→ 1 (pasture)

Nelson Road

Liberty Rd.

2

Hudson Arms Road

Dekker Road

Lowry Rd.

Price Rd.

N. Outlook Road

Cemetery Rd.

Chute Road

Scoon Rd.

x sketch

(97)

GOLDENDALE 48

Snyder Road

Van Belle Road

Nass Rd.

Squash, Squash, Asparagus, Corn

7.1 →

Fordyce Rd.

Cemetery Rd.

Washout Rd.
.9

(241)

(22)

GRANGER

(12)

1 →

North Ave.

1.3

SUNNYSIDE

16th St.

Factory Rd.

Alexander Road

Waneta Rd.

(12)

(not all roads are shown)

(dairy farms)

2.8

Tear Rd.

Yakima River

Stover Rd.

1 ↓

Mabton Sunnyside Road

4.2

↓

(22)

MABTON

23 ↓ to Bickleton

Farm roads along the banks of the Yakima

Apples, plums, asparagus, corn, hops, and grapes are some of the crops that grow along these roads. Hops are derived from a most decorative plant that has green garlands of leaves ten to twenty feet high. I sketch a house seemingly engulfed by grapevines. Premium-quality grapes are grown in Yakima Valley for Washington's fine wines.

Farm roads to Fort Simcoe and also this drive on the east bank of the Yakima River illustrate the agricultural abundance of the great Yakima Valley.

Vineyard near Sunnyside, Yakima County

MABTON

PROSSER 12

YAKIMA 39

Bickleton Road

7.3

expansive view of Yakima Valley

Township Road

.7

Alderdale Road

5

Smith Road

6.2

Naught Rd.

Donoho Road

6.5

see plaque to founder Charles M. Bickle

Horse Heaven Hills

BICKLETON

Goldendale Rd.

Naught Rd.

CLEVELAND

Dot Road

(High plateau land—long views)   19.7

GOLDENDALE ←15.5

Rock Creek Rd.   5.3

← unmarked road

←[97]   18.2

4

2.8

GOODNOE HILLS

sketch

[14]

Columbia River

The road to Bickleton and Rock Creek Canyon

The road winds through the sagebrush of Horse Heaven Hills, affording views of the Yakima Valley, which I am leaving behind.

Past the hamlets of Bickleton and Cleveland, marginal forest land begins. In Rock Creek Canyon the road hugs the creek bed with oaks, alders, and elderberry bushes growing in its narrow corridor.

Leaving Rock Creek Canyon I sketch an abandoned, and slightly tilting, weathered brown house peaking over a barren hillside.

Ghostly house, near Rock Creek Canyon, Klickitat County

The road through Goodnoe Hills and Klickitat Valley

Good views of Columbia River country are along these roads, including the big mountains Hood and Adams. Leaving the Goodnoe Hills I pass fields of grain, hay and sunflowers in the broad Klickitat Valley. I stop to sketch a lonely looking farm.

The Dalles Mountain Road begins here, a slow, bumpy road over the Columbia hills. Once over the ridge I come upon a view that I will never forget. I imagine that I am looking south over the whole state of Oregon, its agricultural patterns continuing to infinity. The road is an exciting one both for its wonderful views and for the thrill of its precipitous mountain drive.

Klickitat Valley landscape, Klickitat County

*View of Mount Adams,
near Glenwood,
Klickitat County*

Back road from White Salmon

Mountain and forest views, green meadows and old farmhouses describe the landscape along this back road. Near Conboy Lake I sketch Mount Adams, a ghostly old farmhouse in the foreground. Glenwood is a lively little town to visit; then I drive toward BZ Corners where I observe the pleasant dairy countryside with its cows, hay crops, and big old barns. It is a good road to end my memorable journey through the beautiful state of Washington.

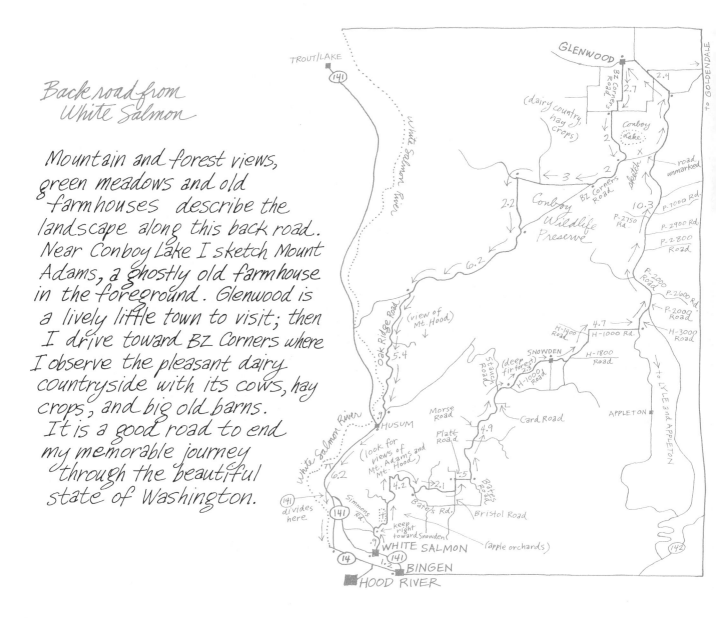

Epilogue

It is my wish that road builders will not straighten and widen our most picturesque back roads. And not even take out all the bumps. It encourages motorists to go ever faster, and to spend less time enjoying the trip. I agree that there must be fast highways and other fast roads, but there are also other roads that need not be.

As an artist, I am particularly concerned with impressions of nature, farmland and architecture. To make each day a series of remembered aesthetic experiences seems to me a happy goal.

As my respect for my fellowman makes me proud to be human, so my respect for nature makes me proud to be part of it.

I wish you many happy travels.

Frog Rock,
Bainbridge Island,
Kitsap County

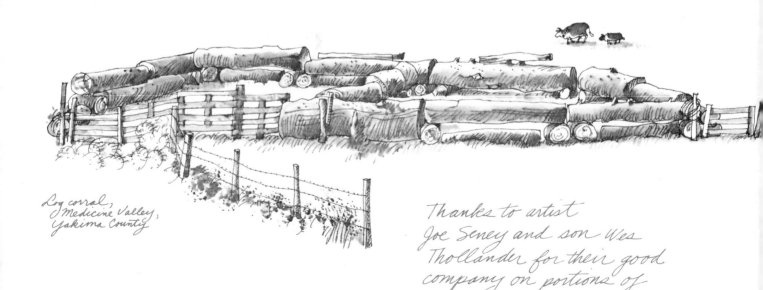

Log corral,
Medicine Valley,
Yakima County

Thanks to artist Joe Seney and son Wes Thollander for their good company on portions of the 6000-mile back road trip through Washington.

200